William Brittlebank

Persia during the famine

a narrative of a tour in the east and of the journey out and home

William Brittlebank

Persia during the famine
a narrative of a tour in the east and of the journey out and home

ISBN/EAN: 9783744798617

Printed in Europe, USA, Canada, Australia, Japan

Cover: Foto ©Andreas Hilbeck / pixelio.de

More available books at **www.hansebooks.com**

PERSIA DURING THE FAMINE.

A WARRIOR OF ADEN.
page 41

PERSIA DURING THE FAMINE

A NARRATIVE OF A TOUR IN THE

EAST AND OF THE JOURNEY

OUT AND HOME

BY WILLIAM BRITTLEBANK

LONDON

BASIL MONTAGU PICKERING

196 PICCADILLY

1873

TO

E. A. D.

WHOSE FRIENDSHIP I DEARLY PRIZE AND HOPE EVER TO RETAIN

THIS UNPRETENTIOUS VOLUME IS

Dedicated

IN AFFECTIONATE REMEMBRANCE OF THE MANY PLEASANT

HOURS WE HAVE SPENT IN EACH

OTHER'S SOCIETY.

THE AUTHOR.

PREFACE.

THE tour, the incidents of which are narrated in the following pages, was made in 1872. Persia was at the time afflicted with famine, and offered little attraction to the traveller. It was, however, out of the beaten track, and this, combined with an Englishman's love for adventure, determined me to return from India to Europe by way of it, the Caspian Sea and the Volga. The character and extent of the famine became painfully evident as I traversed the country from Bushire to Enzelli. It could be traced in every village and town—in the sandy wastes and desert plains. It in consequence forms a prominent feature in my book, the publication of which is due rather to the prompting of friends than to any belief in my own capacity as a writer. I offer it to the public with much diffidence; but I trust that, notwithstanding its many imperfections, it may still be found sufficiently interesting to while away a dull or weary hour. I ought in conclusion to add that when I started on my tour I had no intention of committing my experiences to print. I therefore made few notes, save of the dates of my arrival at and departure from the chief places at which I stopped. The narrative of my travels, such as it is, has been written almost wholly from memory, and this must be my excuse for any errors, especially in the matter of names, into which I may have fallen.

WILLIAM BRITTLEBANK.

May, 1873.

CONTENTS.

Chapter I.
London to Malta . . . 1

Chapter II.
Malta to Suez . . . 14

Chapter III.
Suez to Ceylon 32

Chapter IV.
Point de Galle to Colombo, Kandy, Madras, and Bombay 59

Chapter V.
Madras—Bombay to Bunder Abbas . . 70

Chapter VI.
Bunder Abbas to Bushire . . 87

Chapter VII.
Bushire 95

CONTENTS.

CHAPTER VIII.
Bushire to Burazjoon . . 106

CHAPTER IX.
Burazjoon to Shiraz . . 119

CHAPTER X.
Shiraz . . . 136

CHAPTER XI.
Shiraz to Ispahan . 150

CHAPTER XII.
Shiraz to Ispahan (*continued*) . . 166

CHAPTER XIII.
Ispahan to Resht . . . 190

CHAPTER XIV.
Resht to Enzelli . . 225

CHAPTER XV.
Enzelli to Astrakhan—Nijni Novgorod . . 243

CHAPTER XVI.
Home . . 260

Chapter I.

LONDON TO MALTA.

WEARY of the life I was leading at home—I had left Eton, and felt no inclination for a University career—I resolved to travel. I had already seen most of the Continent of Europe. With France, Belgium, Italy, and Germany I was familiar, having spent many years of my early youth in those countries; and I had also been to Canada and the United States of America. The love of travel was thus early developed in me; and though only in my eighteenth year, I reckoned with confidence on the experience which I had acquired, particularly in my American trip, to carry me successfully through the more distant and ambitious tour which I now contemplated. I had long desired to visit the East. I therefore resolved to shape my course in the first instance for Bombay, and leave it to chance or events to determine whither I should afterwards proceed.

I started from Winster, in Derbyshire, in the latter end of December, 1871, and came to London to make the final arrangements for my journey. These completed, I proceeded to Southampton, and on the 4th January, 1872, got early on board the Peninsular and Oriental Company's steamer bound for Alexandria, in order that I might become familiar with the ship, and be able, without inconvenience, to stow my things in my cabin, which is no easy matter, particularly if you have other passengers in the same room. As good luck would have it I had not; and my kit was also compact, consisting only of two portmanteaus. The smaller of the two I stowed away in the corner of my cabin, and then went on deck to see that the other was placed with the heavier luggage in the hold. I had given it in charge to the hotel-porter, who undertook to bring it to the steamer and have it stowed away, but when I inquired about it, no one seemed to know where it was. I immediately went on shore to see if I could find it, but my most diligent search proved fruitless. As a last resort I called in the aid of my cabin steward, who soon discovered to my no small delight the missing article, which, owing to the carelessness of the porter, had been left in some out-of-the-way place. This incident, trifling in itself, was for the time the cause of much annoyance and anxiety to me, and made me resolve in future never to lose sight of my luggage again. On going on deck with the view of making a tour of inspection of the ship, I found everybody and everything in that state of commotion which invariably attends a departure on a long voyage. Here a knot of passengers were gathered round a boy who was selling books and periodicals He found a ready sale for his wares, but I doubt whether the purchasers derived from them the expected solace and comfort, for the weather was so heavy throughout the whole passage to Gibraltar, that reading was out of the question. Others, again, were taking leave of their friends, struggling hard to conceal the sorrow which lay at their heart, and to comfort those from whom they were about to part by affecting a gaiety which they did not feel. Some of the partings seemed very hard indeed, but were not quite so distressing as those which I witnessed among a body of emigrants, chiefly Irish, on board one of the Inman line of steamers bound for America. It may be that all felt the like grief, and that the difference between them consisted in this—that those whom I now beheld, habituated to self-control, restrained their feelings; while the others, more impulsive, if not more warm-hearted, readily gave way to them. For my own part, I was glad that I had no one to say good-bye to; and I fancied that the emigrant and traveller would leave his native land with a lighter and more hopeful heart if he had not to say "farewell" to dear friends, in too many instances, alas! to some who are nearer and dearer than friends.

The crew were busy in the discharge of their several duties, unmoved and methodical after the fashion of the British tar. Some were taking the covers off the trysails; others were stowing away in the hold the luggage of the late arrivals; whilst over all the din could be heard the hot argument and vehement remonstrance of some elderly gentleman with the steward, on finding, on his return to his cabin, that some one had put a strange portmanteau on his bunk and displaced his own. The very engines seemed in a hurry to be off, and manifested their impatience by moans and hisses. At last everything is ready. The cables are slipped, the vessel is warped off from the quay, the steam is put on gently, and we glide slowly out of dock. On the pierhead a party of people are waving their handkerchiefs and bidding us a last adieu. The steward responds with equal vigour, but not such wet eyes as those on shore, and in a minute more we pass the P. and O. Company's steamship "Peshawa," one of the finest of their fleet, and have fairly commenced our voyage.

About an hour after we had started the wind began to blow hard, and the rain came down in torrents. The captain was on the bridge, enveloped in water-proof from head to foot; by his side the pilot, who was equally well protected against the elements. It becoming rather disagreeable on deck I went below to inquire about dinner. Being told that it would not be ready for some time I got my waterproofs on, and coming again on deck was much surprised to find how the wind had increased. It struck me as a bad beginning to my travels, but I soon remembered that at this time of the year—midwinter—such weather must be expected, and consoled myself with the thought of dinner, the savoury odour of which was already being wafted aft from the cook's galley. On descending into the cabin I found that the stewards were busy laying the tables. The traditional "old traveller," who in every vessel is to be found, let the weather be rough or fine, sitting in the after part of the saloon reading, was in his place; and a few ladies, who were grouped together in another corner, were diligently plying their needles and merging all thought of sea-sickness in their work. A familiar object also met my gaze—I mean the "fiddles." "What are fiddles?" the inexperienced will ask. Let me then explain for the benefit of such, that "fiddles"—"sea-fiddles"—are a species of tray or framework which is attached to the cabin table in stormy weather, and that by means of this framework the cups, plates, dishes, &c. on the table are kept in their places. The appearance of the "fiddle" is always ominous. Very soon those to whom the barometer is a mystery learn to understand the significance of the "fiddle," and when they see it flanking the table know that heavy seas are running. The mizen-mast, which came through the cabin and formed, at the same time, a sort of ornamental pillar, was, with the sides of the saloon, very tastefully decorated with holly. Various other trifles served to show that we had reached the season of year when mirth and jollity become a duty, and altogether the saloon presented a most cheery appearance, especially when the dinner was on the table. In fact, if it had not been for the gentle motion of the ship and the number of strange faces, one might have fancied oneself at home at a Christmas party. The dinner was served in admirable style, and everything was good. Much has been said and written about the style of living on board the P. and O. Company's boats. I have no wish to depreciate it, but, so far as my experience goes, no line of steamers provide a better table for their passengers than the Inman line, on the passage from Liverpool to New York. There was not much conversation during dinner, nearly all present being perfect strangers to each other.

On the dessert appearing things began to improve, conversation became more general, and some of the ladies ventured to ask their *vis-à-vis* at table what sort of weather we were likely to have. They were rather shocked on hearing that in all probability it would be bad, and had not long to wait for the confirmation of their fears. For the wind still increasing, the captain resolved to come to anchor off the Isle of Wight, and remain under its shelter until the weather somewhat moderated. Shortly afterwards I heard the familiar sound of the bell with which the officer on the bridge communicates with those in the engine-room, the engines went almost immediately at half-speed, and then away rushed the anchors, dragging their cables through the hawse-pipes with that rattling noise which at first excites alarm, but which, when the ear becomes accustomed to it, and you are sailor enough to know what it implies, excites the hope of a pleasant run ashore.

We were now at anchor, and it being time for bed, I descended to my cabin and found, as I had expected, that no one was to share it with me. I "turned in," and having got up earlier than usual was soon buried in sleep, which was rendered the deeper by the whistling of the wind through the cordage and the splashing of the water against the ship's side. The next morning I was awoke by the "first bell," and learning that the weather had moderated a little, and that we would start in an hour or so, I cheerfully obeyed the summons of the "second bell," and went down to breakfast, of which I partook most heartily, knowing that it was probably the last meal which I should be able to take with any degree of comfort for a long time. After breakfast we got under way and steamed down the Southampton Waters. On nearing the Needles the sea began to increase perceptibly, and when outside the good ship "Candia,"—(she was one of the Company's old and smaller ships, but made much better weather than many a larger vessel I have seen)—became so lively that it was impossible for a landsman to keep on his feet. One by one the passengers left the deck, cold and heavy rain began to fall, and I descended to my bunk, there to remain in all the agonies of sea-sickness for several days. Knowing that I should be ill I made myself as comfortable as the circumstances would admit of, and resigned myself to fate. The wind increased towards evening and at midnight blew a full gale. What with the noise of the waves dashing against the ship's sides, the heavy steps of the sailors on deck in their big sea-boots, the roaring of the wind through the rigging and the rolling of the vessel in the heavy seas through which she was ploughing her way, I passed a very disagreeable night. I could also hear the working of the engines as they revolved faster or slower according to the depth the screw was immersed in the water, but I always enjoy their sound, which has a certain rhythm, and sleep the sounder for it. Morning dawned at last, and with it the row on deck and on board the ship generally became greater. My steward slipped in for my boots, which I regarded as a piece of humour on his part, feeling assured that I should not have the pleasure of putting them on for some days. He came again with some tea, which was hot and strong. I asked for some milk, but he said it would do me more good if I drank it as it was. I followed his advice, and—never tasted tea any more during the voyage, to such an extent did it upset me. Most travellers profess to have a specific for this most distressing of ailments—*mal de mer*. Some humorists recommend that you should lie flat on your back and think of some one or some thing on shore; others say, lie on your side, and many advise a wrapper tied very tightly round the stomach. My recommendation, based, I regret to say, on a somewhat lengthened experience of sea-sickness, is to lie in the position you find most comfortable (common-sense counsel at least, the reader will admit), to eat liberally, and to avoid brandy however pressed upon you by the stewards. A little sherry and cold water may sometimes be taken, but no matter what the remedy may be it will only afford temporary relief.

About the 7th the weather moderated considerably, but it still blew hard, and the sea kept very rough. I got up and felt much better for the change. Some of the sails were set, and we seemed to be going at a good rate through the water. About 9 P. M. on the 10th January we arrived at Gibraltar; but it being dark I saw nothing of the far-famed rock. We steamed into a sort of harbour amid several ships and some men-of-war; and on coming to anchor the surgeon went ashore to show his bill of health, which I think was clean. The town seemed to be well lighted; but on the whole I should say it is a dull residence. A man-of-war steam launch came alongside for a naval officer we had brought with us, and the mails. The water was very lumpy, and she bobbed about in the most lively manner. The very sight of her movements would have made me feel ill some days before, but now, having crossed the bay, I was able to gaze upon her with the utmost composure. We left Gibraltar about 3 A.M. the next morning, and could see in the distance a beautiful range of snow-capped mountains, which I shall not easily forget. Towards evening, when the sun shed its last rays upon them, the effect was glorious, and filled both mind and eye with a sense of beauty. We experienced fine weather throughout the run to Malta, save on one night, when we encountered one of the terrible squalls to which the Mediterranean is subject. It came down without the slightest warning, and with indescribable fury. The crash in the steward's pantry was awful; it seemed as if all the glass and crockery in the vessel was being smashed. Before the squall struck us we had been going at a good rate and smoothly through the water; now we were madly plunging in a wild sea, which swept clean over the ship. I think it was even a rougher night than any we had experienced in crossing the bay; but I was so far seasoned as to suffer little from it. The night passed, leaving nothing of the storm that had marked it but a smart breeze and a lively sea. Raffles now became the order of the day. The purser got "odds and ends" together, which were about as varied and worthless as the collection of articles at a charity bazaar; for these we raffled, and with this excitement whiled away the time until the 14th January, when we sighted the island of Malta.

Chapter II.

MALTA TO SUEZ.

WE had now entered the harbour of Valetta. Innumerable gondola-like boats, painted at bow and stern all the colours of the rainbow, flitted across its waters and gave to the scene, which was one of the most picturesque I had ever beheld, an air of Venice in carnival time. As we were to coal here, I thought I would make the best of the time at our disposal and visit the town, but hesitated about doing so, when the uproar caused by the competition of the swarthy and dusky native crews for the fares from the steamer reached my ears. They pushed and fought, gesticulated and screamed, in a manner that recalled the monkey-house of the London Zoological Gardens on an Easter Monday. Walking on to the gangway,

I became the object of fierce contention among them. The successful captors bore me to their boat, and before I could well collect my scattered senses, we had reached the shore, where I found several of my fellow-passengers already collected. Among them was one whose acquaintance I had made on the voyage, and with him I proceeded to stroll through the town and climb its quaint, steep streets with their innumerable steps. They are also very narrow, but clean. In fact, I was much astonished to find them so clean, and attributed it to their great incline, which allows the heavy rains to sweep away all the refuse matter which may be cast on them into the sea. The Strada San Giovanni in particular reminded us that we were on the border-land of the East. Its lofty houses afforded a grateful shade from the noontide sun; and the origin of their architecture was further indicated by their projecting windows and balconies and flat roofs. Before travelling in the East I had always fancied when examining the pictures in books of travel in that region, that the dark-eyed beauties represented as sitting in the balconies of the houses, attired in rich silks and gold-embroidered dresses, were put there to fill up the drawing and add to its effect. I had now to correct my judgment; for go where you will in the East, you will find the women perched on the balconies or roofs of their dwellings. There they assemble and gossip, and when seated alone bear an absurd resemblance to the carved images of the saints which are placed in the recesses at the corners of streets in Continental towns.

It is the usual thing for passengers by the P. and O. Company's boats calling at Malta to visit a certain shop where meerschaum pipes and tobacco, pale ale and brandy, are to be had. Having complied with the custom we sallied forth again to see some more of the "lions." We visited Fort Sant' Angelo, from which we had a splendid view of the harbour, where H. M. ship "Marlborough" lay peacefully at anchor, and, indeed, of the whole town, which, with its myriad of flat roofs, grew more and more Eastern in aspect. A drive in a Maltese cart brought us to the principal promenade of the place. There are several such walks, lined with trees on either side, about the town, and here the inhabitants stroll and enjoy themselves in the cool evening air. The horses struck me as being remarkably blood-like. Their legs were as clean as some of our well-bred English horses, and their Arab descent showed itself in their "filbert feet." Wheat and cotton, of which there are often two crops in the year, are the chief products of the island. Its manufactures are cotton goods, jewellery, and cabinet-work, and Valetta is famed for its lace—a fact which our lady passengers seemed fully to appreciate, judging by the quantity of the delicate material which they brought on board with them. It being Sunday, the theatre, which is rather a fine building, was closed, and there being nothing more to detain us, we turned our steps towards the harbour; which, after losing our way several times, we eventually made by the aid of a Maltese boy who spoke a little English. Jumping on board a boat—there were now only about half a dozen at the slip where some few hours before there were as many scores—we told the men to row for their lives to the mail steamer; for it was now late, and we did not know when she was to leave port. However, on nearing her the noise on board was sufficient to assure us that she was still taking in coal, and therefore would not start for some time. It was a beautiful moonlight night, and if it had not been for the coal-dust, a few hours on deck would have been most enjoyable. As it was I got under the lee of one of the sails rigged up for the protection of the quarter-deck, and here ensconced gazed on the harbour and the crowd of silent ships, whose lights were reflected in the water and appeared as varied and countless as those of a Chinese feast. It looked like a scene in a fairy extravaganza. The sea no longer swarmed with boats with chattering crews, its repose was undisturbed. Now and then the gig of a merchant ship might be seen taking the master on board, and the sound of her oars as they dipped in the water alone broke the deep silence which reigned all round. As it grew later, another batch of passengers came on board. One of them had evidently been enjoying himself, and was so elated that he took up one side of the quarter-deck to himself. I confess I was not surprised at it. When I first got ashore myself I felt inclined to jump about and shout, such was my joy at getting free from the narrow compass of the ship; and afterwards reflecting on it, it struck me that, however melancholy or blameable, nothing can be more natural than the boisterous conduct and extravagance of sailors on coming into port after a long cruise.

We steamed away again on our voyage on the 15th about 4 A.M. and, coming later on in the morning on deck, I was rejoiced to find that the awnings had been put up, as they gave it a cosier appearance, and made reading and lounging more agreeable. The voyage had nevertheless become tedious, and I felt, therefore, very glad when the steward came into my cabin and announced that land was in sight. I was soon dressed and on deck. The sun was just rising, and in the far distance we could see the land, which was rather obscured by a belt of haze extending nearly along its whole length. As the mist cleared off we got a better view of the coast, and on approaching nearer, the houses, temples, and domes of Alexandria, on which the sun was now brightly shining, became more distinct. Shortly afterwards the pilot boat could be seen bobbing up and down on the waves. As she approached our engines were eased, and a rope was thrown to those on board the boat, which, after three attempts, they succeeded in making fast. They were dusky-looking fellows, and when we saw their dress, which deprived them of the free use of their legs, we were not surprised at their lubberliness. Soon after shipping the pilot we ran into the harbour, which was filled with vessels flying the ensigns of almost every nation; and, after threading our way through them, came to anchor near the Khedive's yacht, which was built in England, and looked a regular clinking craft. We had not been at anchor above a quarter of an hour before the Peninsular and Oriental Company's paddle steamer "Delta" came steaming in from Brindisi. Her quarter-deck was crowded with passengers, among whom were several ladies. Most of these, in anticipation of the journey across the desert, wore blue veils, while nearly all the male passengers had already donned the "puggary," than which, owing to the thin and light material of which it is composed, nothing can afford less protection against sunstroke. The best contrivance for this purpose is the "solar helmet," which is made of cork, or pith, and the farther it extends over the nape of the neck—the vulnerable point—the better.

As we were not to take the train for Suez until 4 or 5 o'clock in the afternoon, I went ashore to see as much of Alexandria in the interval as I could. Taking one of the rickety carriages which stood outside the custom-house—I was readily allowed to pass through, though without a passport, on representing that I was a passenger per "Candia," bound for India—I drove through the city. In the old and native quarters, the streets, which are narrow like those in all Eastern towns, were covered with mud and refuse from eight to ten inches deep, and from most of the houses there hung tattered and torn matting-awnings, which gave them an air of extreme poverty. The Europeans live in the south-eastern quarter, near the new harbour; and here, where the hotels are also to be found, there is an open square, with wide streets. The contrast presented in the dresses of the people was most striking. Some of the upper classes were habited in the most elegant costumes; but as to the poor, it would be impossible to describe the filth and wretchedness of their garments. Here walked a stately

Bedawee, clothed in woollen shirt and hooded cloak—there a beggar in dirty and scanty rags. Blind and venerable-looking, with a grey beard hanging down almost to his waist, his years and his affliction are no protection to him; for here comes a camel-driver, yelling to all to make way, and roughly jostles the old man aside, laughing at his misery. The camels appeared to share the character of their savage drivers. They are exceedingly obstinate. I have seen one lie down in the middle of the street, so as to prevent those behind from passing, and refuse to rise until its burden was reduced. Donkeys are encountered at every point, and are driven through the streets at a pace which threatens the safety of all foot-passengers. The natives, however, do not seem to mind them; but, on hearing the furious shouts of the boys, quietly look over their shoulders and move out of the way. The water-carriers are also a feature in the scene. With large skins, about four feet long and six feet in circumference, which contain the water, strapped on their backs, they, staff in hand, walk quickly along, and make light of the heavy burden which they carry. One I noticed in particular. He was dressed in a loose shirt, which extended down to his knees, and was fastened at his waist by a leather strap. Round his left leg he wore a ring, which I supposed was his charm; his hair was thick and curly, but cut short; his complexion was dark; and his frame was typical of strength and endurance. Of the beauty of the women of the upper classes I cannot speak, the greater portion of their faces being covered by a white cloth known as the "yashmak." Some few, however, I did see uncovered, and as to them—well, some old London apple-women of my acquaintance might challenge comparison with them, and appeal with confidence to the judgment of Paris.

Leaving this part of the town we drove to Pompey's Pillar, and on the way passed through some beautiful groves of palm-trees. In one of the streets through which our route lay I was startled by a great and indescribable noise. I could not make out what it was until we approached the place whence the cries proceeded, and then the matter explained itself. It was a native funeral. There was the coffin on the bier, in which the dead body reposed. Around it were grouped the friends and relations of the deceased, mourning aloud in turns. I stood some time watching their proceedings, and noticed that while one-half of them were engaged in howling, the other half sat at a short distance off laughing, talking, and eating sweets together. I got out of the carriage with the intention of looking at the corpse, but was dissuaded from carrying my foolish intention into effect by one of the crowd who spoke a little English, and who told me that they did not allow Christians to see their dead. We soon reached Pompey's Pillar, which stands on an eminence not far from the wall of the town and at no very great distance from the Mahmoudie Canal. It is about sixty-eight feet high and nine feet in diameter. The capital is a single block ten feet high, and the substructure, which is about four feet high, is beautifully worked, but disfigured by the names of tourists and other visitors scored and painted upon it. I was told that if any one wants to ascend it the usual method is to fly a large kite, to which some stout cord is attached, over it. The line is thus drawn over the top of the pillar, and when the kite is brought to the ground a stouter line is substituted, and by it the adventurous climber is drawn up the giddy height. It is said that a curious and courageous English lady made the ascent in this way, but I should say that her example is not likely to be imitated. There are numerous pieces of ancient sculpture lying about the base of the Pillar. Some are buried deep in the sand, others lie on the surface, but an examination of them is rendered almost impossible by the stench from the abominations with which the place is surrounded. Talk about the poetry of the East! The loathsome sights which everywhere offend the senses in the neighbourhood of the Pillar are quite sufficient to dispel the idea, and I confess I was glad when I had done this "lion" of Alexandria.

There is another penalty, also, which one has to pay when sight-seeing in this quarter. Crowds of wretched boys pursue your carriage with incessant cries of "backshish" (alms). Give and they will cry for more. If you be wise do at first what you will have to do at last, surrender yourself to the gods of torment and seek refuge in patience.

The tradesmen and merchants seemed to me to be most contented with their lot. They sat on their heels in their shops, which resemble cupboards, made of stone or brick, and are about three feet high and four feet wide. Here they calmly smoked their "hookahs," talking in a lazy, sleepy way to their customers, and apparently indifferent whether they effected a sale or not. The women of the poorer class sit at the street corners and sell bread and dried fruits. Why, by the way, do old women in all parts of the world choose this sort of trade to earn a living, and always exhibit their wares at street corners? I know not what philosophy may underlie this identity of practice on the part of the aged sisterhood, but the fact will be admitted by all travellers. The fee for a guide is five piastres *per diem*, but as is the case with all such persons all the world over, they manage one way or another to get much more out of you. The Khedive's palace, which can be seen by asking for an order from the vakil (steward), is a plain edifice, with inlaid and polished floors. The climate of Alexandria is, however, unhealthy, owing to the conversion of the salt-lake in its neighbourhood into a marsh, and the place in consequence is not much frequented by his Highness. The water is also bad ; fevers are very prevalent, and as a rule, whenever the plague afflicts Egypt it makes its first appearance in the city. That part of the palace devoted to the " harem " is still closed to the male visitor. Its inmates, however, are not as strictly secluded within its limits as they formerly were, and when they visit the shops those who have pretty faces contrive to show them by the use of " yashmaks " of the slightest texture.

The day was now far advanced, so we drove as rapidly as we could to the quay. Jumping into a boat, I was soon at the ship's side, and arrived just in time for dinner, for which I was well prepared, having tasted nothing since I left the boat but some wretched fare at ten o'clock in the morning at one of the hotels, which are both bad and dear. It was certainly most enjoyable to get on board the dear old " Candia " again. It was like jumping at a bound from the East into the heart of England. After dinner all the passengers got their traps ready and came ashore in the tender, which landed us not many yards from the railway station. It is usual, whilst still on board the steamer, to form parties for the journey by railway to Suez. That of which I formed one consisted, besides myself, of an indigo planter on his way to Barrapore, near Terhoot; a coffee-planter going to his plantation near Colombo, Ceylon; an engineer bound for Calcutta; a bank clerk proceeding to Hong-Kong; and a Madras merchant. We found a great many natives selling oranges, and crowds of loafing Arabs at the station. After waiting for about three quarters of an hour, the bell sounded and the guard appeared, shouting as if we had not a moment to spare, "All in!" "Take seats!" pronouncing them as if they were but two words. I could not determine his nationality, but he certainly was not an Englishman. He then disappeared for several minutes, and came back shouting still more vehemently and impetuously the almost unintelligible command. Having repeated it at intervals of some minutes about a dozen times, with the view seemingly of airing his English, and assuring himself that it was obeyed after the passengers had entered, by going round to each carriage and asking "All in" "Take seats?" we slowly glided out of the station, and commenced our journey to Suez, which is about 224 miles from Alexandria. The distance is usually run in ten hours. When the train arrived at Zagazig, which is about half way, the air was extremely cold, in fact it was freezing; yet numbers of Arabs, scantily clad, and with bare feet, were prowling about, not much affected, apparently, by the severity of the weather. After a tedious journey we arrived at Suez, and a few minutes more brought us to the place for embarkation on board the Peninsular and Oriental Company's boats. During the railway trip I had altered my plans, and resolved, instead of going on to Bombay, to proceed in the first instance to Ceylon. Running the gauntlet through a swarm of donkey-boys who had to be kept in order by a smartish rap or two with my stick, I selected one of their animals and started off for the office of the Company's agent, which was some three miles distant, and lay on the other side of a sandy plain. I soon reached my destination, the donkey going at a rate which surprised me, and not even slackening its pace as we dashed through the bazaar of Suez.

The town, which is in a state of rapid development, bids fair to be the most important seaport of Egypt. Not many years since little better than a village, it has now a population of some 7,000 native and about 3,000 European inhabitants. It does not however boast of many buildings of note. The principal ones are the Mosque, the Hospital for Pilgrims, the Custom House, and the Peninsular and Oriental Company's Offices. I was told that there was also a British Military Hospital in course of erection, but I did not see it. Originally the water and provisions for its use had to be fetched from Cairo, which is about seventy miles distant by rail. It is now abundantly supplied with sweet water; and the completion of the ship-canal across the isthmus must ultimately increase its wealth and commercial importance. The length of the canal, exclusive of sixty-two miles of lakes through which it passes, from the Mediterranean to the point at which it discharges itself into the Red Sea, is 100 miles. Its greatest width at the water-line is 328 feet; but for about twenty miles of its course the width is only 196 feet. The width at the bottom is 72 feet all the way, and its depth is about 26 feet. The greatness of the work or its vast utility cannot now be denied. About ten miles to the west of Suez is the mountain range called "Zebel Attaka." The mountains are dry and arid-looking, and are about 2,900 feet above the sea level. The town itself is built on a low sandy desert. In the summer months the heat during the day is terrible, and the glare from the sun is such that the use of spectacles is essential for the protection of the eyes. Having easily changed my ticket for Bombay to one for Point de Galle, Ceylon, I again mounted my donkey, and galloping through the streets and bazaar at the same rate at which I had made my entry, to the imminent risk of many stately Arabs and Turks who, even when struck by the horse of the traveller, never utter a word of remonstrance, but get out of the way as best they can, I soon reached the jetty. After my luggage had been stowed away on board the steamer, I changed my clothes and had a bath, and, what I needed much more, my dinner; and so refreshed I was prepared for our voyage down the Red Sea.

Chapter III.

SUEZ TO CEYLON.

WAS now on board the "Indus," as splendid a ship as any captain could command, and manned by as motley a crew as could be well brought together. On seeing them one might imagine himself on board one of Captain Mayne Reid's "pirates," if it were not for the great size of the vessel. In the afternoon about 4 or 5 o'clock, it became apparent that we should soon start. A number of Arabs stood ready on the quay to assist in our departure, and made a frightful din as they hauled away at the cables. When we got clear they set up a howl, which, though meant for a cheer, had the opposite of an inspiring effect. The next day passed without anything to relieve the monotony of the voyage. Sunday followed. After breakfast the whole crew, with the ex-

ception of those engaged at the time in working the ship, were mustered aft. Dressed in their best clothes they formed a line from the "companion-hatch" to the stern, and back to the hatch again, at many points standing two and three deep, and presented a most picturesque appearance. They included Negroes, Malays, Hindoos, Chinamen, Manilla men, Indians, and representatives of one or two other nations. The Chinamen generally man the captain's gig when the ship is in harbour. At sea they take the helm in turns with the Manilla men, and are said to make excellent sailors. They certainly look very smart, and are most handy in the management of boats. The rest of the crew were all "fine-weather" sailors, three of them being counted as equal to one Englishman. When they had all mustered, the chief officer called over their names, which sounded wonderfully alike, and having answered to the call they were summoned forward by the boatswain's whistle and dismissed. The seats for church were then arranged on deck, the desk was formed by placing cushions over one of the sky-lights, the English ensign was spread over the cushion, and the bell having tolled, the captain proceeded to read the service, which I think is never more impressive than when heard at sea. Church over, the day passed as usual, or perhaps a little more wearily, inasmuch as all abstain from the amusements by which the monotony of the voyage on the other days of the week is relieved.

The great and almost intolerable heat experienced in sailing through the Red Sea is known to all Indian travellers. On board the steamers every contrivance is used to mitigate it. In the "Indus," on the main-deck, which was flush, there were two large ports, about six and a-half feet square, forward. These were always kept open during fine weather, and allowed a current of fresh air to circulate through the ship. I often used to sit near them, and found the place more agreeable than on deck. Further aft came the engines, on each side of which were the berths and the engineers' state-rooms. In the engine-room there was a very good invention designed by the engineers themselves, for causing a "punkah" to sway about without being pulled by any of the crew. Instead of being worked by hand it was connected with a part of the engine by a series of wheels, over which a cord was passed. The "punkah" was thus kept continually in motion, and the engineers had always some air in their cabins although so near the engines. Behind the engines were two more ports about the same size as those forward, and here also the purser's room, the steward's pantry and the bar were placed. The stewards consisted of Englishmen and Indians. Dressed in neat blue-black trousers, short jacket of the same material, left open in front and displaying plenty of clean white shirt, and with a sash or belt around their waists, they looked exceedingly smart and answered the many calls made on them with an alacrity which would have disgusted a west-end footman. The saloon, a magnificent room, was furnished in a style of Oriental luxury, and was kept cool by "punkahs" which were worked from the deck. It is scarcely necessary to say, that the "punkah" is a contrivance by which the air is made to circulate. It is a long piece of cloth, some twenty or twenty-five feet long, and about four feet broad, without reckoning the fringe. It is suspended so as to allow it to swing backwards and forwards, and is kept in motion by one of the crew. It thus makes and wafts a current of air, without which life between decks would be insupportable. On the deck, which was also flush, the scene was of a different character. Here, when the weather was fine, the passengers sat, talked, and made merry; or, taking up their quarters forward of the cabin-hatch, enjoyed themselves in smoking. At night, looking down through the engine sky-light, one might fancy himself not far from the regions of the damned, such was the glare and such the roar of the furnaces in the very depth of the ship, and so discordant was the harsh grating of the shovels and bars as they were trailed over the ash-strewn iron floor. Hot though it was, the negroes generally took up their quarters over the stoke-hole. Others of the crew when they had nothing to do lay down forward at full length. Some sang, if howling be considered singing; some laughed and chatted in groups, and others, acting as barbers, shaved their comrades' heads, which when denuded of their locks resembled a black pig's back. Most of them wore rings on their big toes—a fashion, it struck me, as uncomfortable as ridiculous.

We had a heavy head sea and a strong wind from the same direction right away to the Straits of Bab-el-Mandeb, near which, opposite the telegraph station, is Shadwin Island, where the Peninsular and Oriental Company's steamer "Carnatic" was wrecked on the 13th September, 1869, and thirty lives lost, together with specie, mails and cargo. The Red Sea, from one end to the other, is about 1,100 miles long, by 90 to 150 miles in breadth, with a depth of 400 feet. It has many dangerous coral reefs of great size, which are usually from twenty to twenty-five feet above the surface of the sea, and the prevailing winds in it blow from October to May from S.S.E., and from June to October from N.N.W. Two large rocks, called the "Brothers," are seen about thirty-six hours after leaving Suez; and Zoulla, which was the base of the Abyssinian expedition, is also passed. The island of Perim, which stands a good height above the sea-level, and on which there is a lighthouse, is likewise a conspicuous object on the voyage. We saw very few ships—indeed, the only craft which we did meet were Arabian or Egyptian boats, and we reached Aden about 3 A.M. on the 26th January. Coming on deck later on in the morning, I found that we were coaling, and were surrounded by a number of natives in canoes, about seven or eight feet long. The water seemed to be as much their element as the land. Crying out, "I dive, I dive, I dive!" as an inducement to the passengers to throw a piece of money into the sea, they would suit the action to the word, and catch the coin before it reached the muddy bottom. Several of them dived right under the ship, coming up again on the other side, for a rupee. Approaching close to the ship's side, they would place the palms of their hands against her, then spring as high out of the water as they could, go down feet foremost, and come up at the other side of the ship in about a minute, in the midst of the canoes and coal lighters. Several of them swam from the shore to where we lay, a distance of more than a mile, and after paddling about the ship and diving for a couple of hours, swam back again with evident ease. Their heads seemed wonderfully hard. They beat each other on them with the canoe paddles, and seemed in no way the worse for the knocks, which could be distinctly heard on board the steamer. They are very thin, but at the same time muscular, and those of them whose heads are not shaved, show a crop of thick, reddish-yellow hair. They have a peculiar way of dancing, and beat time either with the feet or by slapping themselves on the arms, chest and thighs. We made them understand that we should like to see them swim a race round the ship. It took some time to arrange the start, as the canoes also wanted to take part in the contest. When off, the biggest of the squad got ahead very soon, but directly the little ones found they stood no chance, they dived under the ship, so that when the big fellows were rounding the cut-water, the others were nearly at the winning-post. A canoe race also took place, and caused much more excitement, several of the frail craft being swamped, but righted again with marvellous skill and quickness by their crews.

Aden is situated on a barren, rocky, arid peninsula, surrounded by hills and extinct volcanoes. Breakfast over, I got into a boat and was pulled ashore, intending to visit the "tanks," of which I had heard much. As it was very hot, although in the month of January, I took a carriage and drove first to the hotel, which is built on a kind of terrace at the edge of the beach. Its accommodation is good, and its billiard-table, I fancy, is the only amusement open to our military officers stationed at the place. Leaving the hotel, we rattled away across the dry ground towards the "tanks," around which alone throughout all Aden are to be seen signs of vegetation. There are several of them, and they are used for storing up the rain-water which falls in this part of the world only on rare occasions. At the date of my visit there had not been rain for nearly two years previously, and sometimes it does not fall for an interval of three years. At one time the tanks were allowed to become filled with sand and rubbish, but they have been cleared and repaired, and are now capable of containing an enormous quantity of water.

The natives looked a ferocious and inhospitable set of people. Most of them wore only loin cloths, and the children were quite naked; but the women were profusely decked with ear-rings and gold ornaments passed through the nose, a simple shirt, however, being their chief clothing. In a stretch of some five or six miles, we passed about 200 or 300 camels. Some were heavily laden; others only bore a stately Arab, with his gun slung over his shoulder and a long knife gleaming at his waist. Others again carried women, who displayed their limbs without any sense of shame, and clumps of brown and dirty children hung on as they best could to the heavily laden beasts. Now and then we encountered a "warrior," whose evident ferocity, not less than his varied arms, betokened his trade. One of them, who looked some forty years of age, was fully six feet three inches in stature. Black as a crow, his body was covered with a white cloth, which was wrapped round him and secured at the waist by a belt. Over this he wore another mantle of different material—it was apparently made of camel's hair—having broad white and brown stripes, with a fringe hanging from the edge, and his feet were covered with sandals, made of hide, and secured by a leather thong passed over the instep. In his belt a huge and ugly knife was stuck. On his left arm he bore a shield about three feet in diameter and perfectly round, and with his left hand he grasped two light spears, which might be thrown as a javelin or retained as a lance. In his right hand he carried a stick of slight dimensions, but loaded at one end with a ball of heavy metal. It struck me that if suddenly attacked he might find some difficulty in determining which of his weapons he would first use. At the same time I should not much relish an encounter with him, not only because of his great size and strength, but also because practice had probably taught him instinctively to seize that one of his many implements of destruction most fitting for the occasion. In 1837 an English merchant vessel from Madras was plundered on the coast. In retaliation, the East India Company captured and took possession of Aden, and when in 1858 the Sultan of Adhlee, which is about twenty miles distant, attempted to stop the supplies to the settlement, he was encountered and severely punished for his temerity by the British commandant. The coast of Arabia can be seen from Aden, looking very dry and flat, but it is not safe to visit it. Several English officers, who some years since attempted to land on it for the purpose of sport, were murdered by the inhospitable and barbarous inhabitants. On returning to the steamer, I found several odd-looking creatures selling what appeared to be ostrich feathers to the ladies. They were bare-footed and wore a petticoat of thin linen, with stripes of a different colour at the top. Besides the petticoat, they wore as an upper dress a night-gown with sleeves, and fringed at the wrists with a kind of braid, and on their heads a round hat of coloured straw, which looked exceedingly like a saucepan *minus* the handle, and on which were stained various devices. They allowed their beards to grow, and had two solitary curls hanging down on each side of the face, but shaved the rest of the head. They are reputed inveterate thieves, and it was with difficulty that the ship was cleared of them.

Having finished coaling we once more resumed our voyage and whiled away the time by whist, chess, and " sea-quoits," which are made of pieces of rope fashioned into a circle and spliced together. I looked out with hope and expectation for the Constellation known as the " Southern Cross," but was unfortunate in never getting a sight of it. We had a good deal of thunder, and of lightning of a very brilliant kind. It was beautiful to watch it at night as it darted from cloud to cloud and lit up the heavens with its vivid flashes. Sometimes it seemed as if it struck the sea. Then would come an interval of inky darkness, and when the thunder-clap was again followed by a flash of brilliant light the whole deck would be illumined and a weird aspect imparted to every object on it. We had one source of suffering. The ship was infested with cockroaches, and the state cabins were at times unbearable with them. Towards 11 A.M. on the morning of the tenth day from Aden we sighted Ceylon. As we drew nearer to the island I could perceive that the forests, which consisted chiefly of cocoanut trees, extended down to the very water's edge. Here and there a cluster of bamboo huts could be seen, some on the banks of little lagoons which sparkled amid the gaudy and luxuriant tropical vegetation, others buried deep in the forest and but in part revealed. On the beach a number of native fishermen were drawing in their nets, and far in the background arose mountains—Adam's Peak towering above all its companions—which stretched away to the right and left and looked clear and blue in the distance. The sea, for seven or eight miles around, was covered with native fishing boats, and the whole scene was full of an enchanting beauty. It being too late to enter the harbour we came to an anchor outside, and from where we lay could see the masts of the Peninsular and Oriental Company's steamer "Rangoon," which had drifted on to the rocks. At night a light was shown from one of the masts to warn the other shipping of her position and their danger. But what a contrast between the beautiful island on which we now gazed and the arid and barren lands which only a few days since we had left! Set in an emerald green sea of such transparency that one could see far down into its depths, teeming with varied and luxuriant vegetation, and with a balmy air laden with delicious odours, to breathe which was a pleasure in itself, I could almost fancy as I looked on it for the first time, and listened to the faint, half-musical sounds which came wafted to us from the shore, that it was one of those enchanted islands of which we read in Eastern story, and that when the morning came we should find no trace of it. Soon all was bustle and life on board the steamer. Every one seemed to have forgotten the weariness of the voyage, and looked forward with pleasure to the prospect of a run ashore in the morning. The present enjoyment was also great. The ship no longer rolled with the swell of the sea, walking was possible, and conversation could be carried on with comfort; and so agreeable was the change that all remained upon deck to an unusually late hour, and at last descended to their cabins with reluctance. For myself I packed up my traps before turning in, and, finding sleep impossible, again got out of my berth and looked through the cabin "port" at the sea as it dashed against the rocks, or listened to the "soughing" of the wind through the rigging of a large ship which lay a short distance from us. The next morning I was up early and was just in time to see the harbour as we entered it. The name "Point de Galle," or "Cock's Point," was given to it by the Portuguese. It affords tolerably safe anchorage at all times of the year, but a heavy swell usually sets in during the S.W. monsoon, which blows from June to September. It is the coaling station of the different steamship companies trading to China, Japan, and Australia, and is therefore annually frequented by a great number of coal ships. In the form of a bay, it is beautifully situated, and is at all times covered with canoes, the largest of which resemble the " flying proa" of the Ladrone Islands. The hull of these boats is dug out of a log of wood, with sides built of boards, and they are so narrow that they would capsize if it were not for an outrigger which keeps them in an upright position. The thwarts are placed on the top of the gunwale, in order to keep those on board of them as much out of the water as possible. They sail very fast, especially with the wind on the quarter, or a little more abeam, and are steered from the lee side with a paddle. We had not been at anchor many minutes when a juggler came off from the shore to us. Directly he got on board he began to display his skill, and performed several very ingenious tricks, one in particular with a mock alligator made of flannel, which could not be surpassed by Houdin or the " Wizard of the North."

Some of the passengers were going on to Colombo, the capital of Ceylon, by one of the British India Company's boats. I preferred to go up by the mail-coach instead, by which means I should see the country much better. Taking a last look at the "Indus," of which I still preserve an agreeable recollection, I got into a canoe, and the wind being fair soon reached the quay. Here my luggage was seized by a couple of natives, who were about to bolt with it even before I had settled with the canoe-men. A few taps with my stick moderated their zeal; and having paid the canoe-men about a quarter of what they demanded, I directed my now submissive porters to shoulder my traps. Emerging from the custom-house, I proceeded along a beautiful avenue lined with trees, with houses on the right and the harbour to the left. Some distance up I passed a guard-house, which was occupied by English soldiers, in spotless white uniforms and solar helmets; and in about five minutes afterwards, reached the Peninsular and Oriental Hotel, on whose spacious terrace a crowd of passengers from our own ship and one that had also arrived from the Mauritius, were gathered. They were not enjoying themselves, as one might imagine they would be after a long voyage, but were engaged in warfare with swarms of natives, who sought by every harassing device to induce them to purchase sticks of a very hard wood, which when let fall vertically on a piece of stone sounds like iron; and other articles peculiar to the island. The hotel itself is a handsome-looking building. It has a very large dining-room and a good billiard-room, and the bed-rooms, airy and clean, have no ceilings, but one common roof, which is a capital arrangement for houses in the tropics. Meeting some of my fellow-passengers, we hired a "bandy," a kind of four-wheeler, which looked like a cross between a London "growler" and a country cart, and drove to the Cinnamon Gardens. On returning, I bought some ivory, which was already sawn into knife-handles, from a native. The transaction was not completed in a moment. It ran this course. Ivory offered for twelve rupees (about £1 4s.). I turned away, and walked towards the carriage. Offer reduced to ten rupees. I got into the carriage. Falling to seven rupees, I told the coachman to drive on; and then came, "I let you have for one rupee." I gave him the rupee and took the ivory. A girl with a splendid head of hair now passed. We told the coachman to ask her what she would take for one of her tresses. "One rupee," was the reply, without the slightest hesitation. So I bought the tress, thinking that the purchase would be welcome at home. These incidents were sufficient to convince me that Point de Galle had become one of the "show places" of the world, and that its inhabitants were well qualified to sustain its new character.

Having accompanied my companions, who were bound for China, to the harbour, I strolled back to the hotel, and arrived in time for dinner. It was very good on the whole. The pine-apples were delicious, and the bananas, which are called plaintains when they are a little larger, most luscious. They are about five or six inches long and one in diameter. The skin which covers the rind is of a yellow colour, with dark purple spots, and tolerably thick, but is easily peeled off. The tree on which they grow is generally from fifteen to twenty feet high, with leaves almost six feet long and two feet broad; the stem is soft and herbaceous, and the fruit, which forms the chief sustenance of the inhabitants of most tropical climates, grows in bunches varying in weight from twelve pounds upwards. We had also for dessert some oranges, not red as we get them at home, but green, and of poor flavour. The spirituous liquor which is principally drank in the island is known as "arac" and is chiefly used as punch. The word "arac" is indeed the Indian name for all strong waters; and whisky, brandy, &c. are called "English arac." It is the juice of the cocoa-nut tree, and is manufactured in the following manner. In the evening, the operator or collector of the juice ascends the tree, taking with him a certain number of round earthen pots with necks. Reaching the branches of the tree, he takes his knife, cuts off the small knobs, and applies the mouths of the bottles to the wounds, fastening them so that they may receive the juice as it exudes from the tree. In the morning he again ascends the tree, and finds most of the bottles full of juice, which is poured into a receptacle prepared for it. This process is gone through for several days, until the requisite quantity of juice is collected, when it is all poured into one vessel and left to ferment. When the fermentation has ceased, and it has become rather tart, it is put into a still and allowed to work as long as that which flows over has any taste of spirit. This, the last product, is very poor and weak, and has to be immediately rectified to prevent its spoiling. The palms which produce the nuts are very numerous in Ceylon, but they only grow near the sea. From Point de Galle to Colombo the way is lined with them. They grow to a height of from sixty to ninety feet. The stem is rather larger at the top and bottom than in the middle, the bark is smooth, of a pale brown colour, and the tree generally leans to one side. The leaves or branches, of which there are from sixteen to twenty-four on each tree, are about fifteen feet long and of a yellowish colour, and taper towards the end. The nuts lie in clusters of about ten each on the top of the tree, and the husk of the nut, which consists of a rough strong fibre, is formed into coir, much used in the East in making mats. Rice is also one of the staple products of the island; and tobacco, which is called "dunkol," meaning leaf, is likewise grown. There are two kinds of "dunkol." One is termed "single dunkol," the other "dunkol kappada." The "kappada" tobacco is much the stronger. Both kinds are produced by the same plant; but while the one is neglected the other is much cared for by the Cingalese. Hence the difference in quality between them. The natives chew the "kappada" with their "betel," and also smoke it, but not through pipes. They take one of the leaves of the plant, roll it, and cover it with the leaf of the wattukan tree, and then smoke it like an ordinary cigar. Betel chewing, to which they are addicted, is assuredly a most disgusting practice. The plant grows like ivy, and like ivy is parasitical, being mostly found twisted round large trees. Its leaves are long and pointed (something like ivy leaves, only softer) and full of red juice. It is much esteemed by the natives, as it renders the breath sweet, colours the lips red, and while preserving the teeth makes them also black, which is considered a mark of beauty. The quantity of it consumed is almost incredible. Every one carries a box of it, which, on the approach of a friend, is handed to him, as we do snuff. Some of them also chew the areca nut, either alone or mixed with the betel leaf and lime; but the areca nut and lime are bad for the teeth. The women use a good deal of betel; and when the natives visit each other, they are invariably regaled with it. It is mostly used after dinner, to prevent sickness, as they say. The only occasions on which they abstain from it are on the funeral day of a relation, or their days of fasting.

After dinner, as it was a little cooler, I sallied forth to see the town. Turning to the right I found myself in what seemed to be the European quarter. Entering a store kept by a Parsee, I purchased a solar helmet, which in shape rather resembled a sou'wester, protruding one or two inches in front and a good many behind, thus affording ample covering for the nape of the neck. It was very light for its size, and I soon became accustomed to it, and used it constantly on my subsequent travels. Keeping on a straight course I again arrived at the sea, and was just in time to see the China steamer sailing out of harbour with my friends on board. I watched her for some time, half wishing that I also had gone with her. She had hardly disappeared when the Australian mail-boat also started on her lonely voyage. Returning to the hotel, I had a game of billiards and then turned in, but not to sleep. I had just become drowsy when I heard the well-known buzz of the mosquito. Having tried in vain to protect myself from their annoyance by lighting the candle and placing my head under the sheet, the only covering on the bed, I jumped up boiling with rage and bathed in perspiration, and seizing a towel, which I first damped, went in for wholesale slaughter of the irritating insects. This accomplished, a lizard creeping up the wall, and gorging itself with flies, dispelled all my drowsiness, and sleep did not close my weary eyes for several hours. While I lay awake I could hear the thunder rattle and see the lightning flash. Such atmospheric disturbance is common to the island. There was not a day during my stay in which I did not witness it. Next morning, after having had a tub and breakfast, I bent my steps in the direction of the "Pittah," or native town. And here I may remark that the roads in Ceylon are about the best in the world. They are as smooth as if they had been watered and rolled for a century, and their colour, which is mostly of a beautiful red, strikingly contrasts with the luxuriant foliage of the trees by which they are shaded. The native huts— they cannot be called houses—are mostly built of bamboo, with leaves for the roofs. Some are built of mud on a platform of the same substance; and this style of dwelling is the most common in the East.

The religion of the Cingalese is a compound of several systems, and makes them very superstitious. On a child being born they immediately call in an astrologer, who is asked to discover whether it will have a prosperous or an unsuccessful life. If he prophesy that its life will not be a prosperous one, they sometimes go so far as to destroy it. A white man, or a woman with child, if seen by a native in the morning, betokens good luck to him; the sight of a cripple or a beggar, on the other hand, is a bad omen. They further believe that they are continuously surrounded by demons. If they are taken ill, or any misfortune befalls them, they attribute it to the demons; and to guard against them they wear various kinds of amulets, and also employ charms and spells. Even those of them who have been converted to the Christian faith still labour under their original terror of the demons, although knowing that they are delusions; and the hill natives are so steeped in this superstition, that many of them are driven to madness by their ignorant fears. Their priests, who are bound to temperance and chastity, and who never eat anything that has had life, are dressed in a large yellow piece of cloth, which is folded round the body and secured by a belt. The right shoulder, the feet, and the head and arms are bare. In one hand they carry a cane, and in the other an umbrella, which is made of the broad end of the "taliput leaf," a gigantic palm with immense fan-shaped leaves. In the temples images of men are seen in different postures and dressed like priests. Some are seated cross-legged with bushy heads of hair; others are in a recumbent position. The temples dedicated to the "inferior gods" are poor and mean-looking, many of them being made of clay and wood, whilst those dedicated to Buddou or Buddah are magnificent in their structure. At the doors of the inferior temples little earthenware pots are placed for the offerings of those who pass; and here also a priest sits all the day, no doubt to guard the contents of the vessels. Inside the temples there are numerous carved figures and gigantic models (not very correct) of beasts and birds, and indecent representations of men and women. The festivals in honour of Buddou are not held in the temples where he is usually worshipped, but on a high mountain in the interior of the island, or on Adam's Peak, which is about forty miles to the northeast of Colombo. On the top of Adam's Peak the "bogaha," a tree held sacred in Ceylon, grows, and under it the worshippers of Buddou hold their festivals, believing that the deity is more partial to their ceremonies when performed under its shade, beneath which lie the remains of ninety native kings. The Brahmins worship a tree called the "banyan;" and all believe that immediately after death the souls of the good assume the rank of gods, whilst those of the wicked become beasts and reptiles. The Cingalese are predestinarians; but they nevertheless imagine that calamities may be mitigated, if not entirely averted, by charms, spells, and offerings. The native priests dread much the spread of the Christian religion in the island, knowing well that in face of the enlightenment and civilization which follow in its train they can no longer practise on the superstitious fears of their countrymen.

Chapter IV.

POINT DE GALLE TO COLOMBO, KANDY, MADRAS, AND BOMBAY.

N the 7th February, at 7 o'clock in the morning, I started for Colombo in the Galle and Colombo "Wain," renowned for its not altogether safe mode of progression. Drawn by two horses which are changed at certain stations, it performs the journey between Galle and Colombo, a distance of eighty miles, at fair speed, and travels over a road as smooth and level as asphalte. The way is lined with beautiful tropical trees; and numerous native huts, with now and then a temple of the inferior kind, are also passed. Sometimes through the foliage a glimpse of the sea is obtained, lending a fresh charm to the scene. The road along its whole length was crowded

with people, some travelling on foot, others in the native "bandie," drawn by diminutive oxen, which can go at the rate of seven miles an hour, and keep it up for twelve or fourteen miles. Priests in their yellow garments also swelled the throng, and occasionally a humble trader might be seen carrying fish or fruit in baskets which are balanced at each end of a bamboo pole placed across the shoulder. In order to advance at any rate of speed with this contrivance, the bearer has to go at a half-walk, half-trot, on account of the springing of the bamboo; and to keep better swing he marks the time by a cry at every other step. Strangest feature of all, during the nine hours we were on the journey we saw no less than twenty-five marriages in course of celebration. We also passed a great many cripples and blind people, and others who seemed to suffer from that horrible and loathsome disease, "elephantiasis." The legs of the wretched beings so afflicted could not have been much smaller than those of an elephant, and the odour from them was most disagreeable. I was told that when the disease began to show itself outwardly, it was already fully established in the system, and that at certain stages of the malady the victim lost nose, hands, and feet. Lepers were also numerous. Our pace was about nine miles per hour, all other vehicles on the road giving way to us at the sound of the horn of the guard, whose powers of jumping on to his seat whilst we were at full speed were something to be noted and admired. Coach-travelling is much patronised by the natives, but their presence is rendered most disagreeable by their habit of betel chewing. After passing many fine cinnamon plantations and dwellings of European inhabitants —some of these houses, placed behind small artificial sheets of water, and surrounded by magnificent trees, looked like scenes in a pantomime—we approached Colombo about half-past four o'clock in the afternoon. The driver, who by the way was a stray Russian, then gave his team an extra flip of his whip, and dashing at a good round pace down the road which leads to the beach, we were soon at the door of the hotel, where I dismounted.

Having secured a room, I sat down to dinner, but being provided with no servant of my own, as most of the other guests were, I suffered much in the matter of waiting. No exception could be taken to the dinner itself, or indeed the general service of the hotel, which may account for its being largely frequented by the residents in the neighbourhood, and the curries were superior to any I afterwards had in India. After dinner, as it was already quite dark, I contented myself with sitting on the verandah and listening to the gentle wash of the sea, which was about thirty yards off, or watching the brilliant and incessant play of the lightning. Fire-flies were also flitting about and looked very pretty as they darted to and fro through the thick vegetation; and later on, the lights of carriages coming to take away visitors from the hotel marked the course of the roads leading to the town. These carriages, by the way, are exceedingly well appointed, and carry a sort of canvas hood, which can be put up in the day time as a shelter against the fierce rays of the sun. The driver and footmen are neatly dressed in white, with a red sash round the waist, and turbans of different colours on the head, and give an air of elegance and completeness to the "turn-out," which would not discredit the drive in Hyde Park. Thanks to a spacious bed-room and a perfect mosquito net, I passed a good night, and rose early next morning that I might have ample time to see the town, which lay rather more than a quarter of a mile from the hotel across a grass common. Walking along the esplanade, I reached the European part of the town, where are situated the merchants' houses, banks, stores, barracks, &c. I found it exceedingly hot, the little air which comes from the ocean as you walk along the esplanade, being completely shut out. I felt almost suffocated, and though my clothes were of the lightest, also suffered from profuse perspiration. On the common, on a site which commands a beautiful view of the sea, and catches the evening breeze which generally begins to blow after sun-set, a new club-house was in course of erection, and behind it at some distance is a lake in which the natives bathe and wash clothes all day long. They do not proceed with the former operation as we do, but going into the water until it reaches their arm-pits, they come to a stand and then pour the water over their heads out of an earthenware jug. Their washing is done by striking the shirt or other article on a flat stone, and must make every European who sees it tremble for his buttons. The harbour, or rather bay, lies on the west side of the town, and there is also a roadstead, which however is only safe during the north-east monsoon. Only very light vessels can approach the wharves, owing to the shallowness of the water—a great drawback, as it necessitates the landing in barges of the cargoes of large ships. Further, for six months of the stormy season this side of the island is subject to heavy rains, accompanied by dreadful thunder and lightning. During this period the variation of the temperature is very great. The rains, which mostly descend at night, render the air damp and chill, and these are followed in the day time by heat which is so excessive as to be almost unbearable. The "Pittah," or black town, is very extensive. During the business hours it swarms with people of every description and colour, and the shops are full of all kinds of articles of merchandize in use among the natives of India. The population includes representatives of almost every race in the East, and like the Chinese numbers of the inhabitants live in bamboo huts built on flat-bottomed boats, which are fastened to the shore in long rows. A peculiar kind of dried fish is to be had here as well as in India. They are called "Bombay ducks," and when the taste for them is acquired are agreeable eating, especially when broken up with curry and rice.

Leaving Colombo, I went up by railway to Kandy to see the coffee districts. Passing through thick forests and over swampy rice-fields, and by herds of oxen and fierce buffaloes, which are used for ploughing, we began to ascend by a steep gradient, which made me feel apprehensive for the safety of the train, running at one point by the side of a cliff several hundred feet in height, and having on the other side, only a few feet from the rails, an abyss of terrible depth. Right away down in the valley a few huts could just be seen; in front densely wooded mountains towered aloft, and assumed in the far distance one uniform colour of magnificent blue. Here and there spaces were cleared for the cultivation of the coffee plant. The planters' houses and stores were all beautifully situated, and the whole scene was so cheerful and full of beauty that the eye dwelt on it with ever-increasing pleasure. At the stations there was the usual hubbub. Plantains and cocoa-nuts were offered for sale by women and children, and were largely consumed by the native passengers. The cocoa-nuts, which they open very dexterously with a knife, are eaten when barely mature. I tried one of them, but felt so sick after it that I did not repeat the experiment. Arrived at Kandy, I strolled to the lake, which is about one mile in circumference, and watched the natives bathing for some time. After the bath they rub themselves all over with cocoa-nut oil, which gives to their skin a most glossy appearance. The practice is an offensive one, but it is said that it makes the limbs supple, and protects the skin from being blistered by the sun. A visit to the temple, which is supposed to contain the tooth of Buddah—the tooth was, by the way, destroyed by the Portuguese, so that the relic now on exhibition must be a sham one—followed, and I then strolled back to the hotel over a grass plot, on which in the cool of the evening the half-castes of the place play at cricket, and the inhabitants walk about at their leisure.

Hearing at the hotel that there were to be races got up by the planters in the neighbourhood the next day, I engaged a seat on the coach which was to start for the scene in the morning. During the night, and indeed for several nights after the races, the guests at the hotel were exceedingly noisy, and bets were made and settled in a way which excited a profound disgust in a gentleman present, who boasted of an acquaintance with Tattersall's. The coach came round early next morning. The driver had that in his eye which, in American phrase, seemed to say, " I can drive round that corner at ten miles per hour and just chip it ; " and he verified his character, taking us to the course, and particularly down the inclines, at a rate which made the natives stare and his passengers tremble. The course was a stiff one, with several ascents and descents. It was well railed out all round, and was lined with natives whose dresses were of the most varied hues. The horses were on the whole a good lot of animals. Some had a great deal of the Arab about them, whilst others were big, raw-boned Australians, which looked as if they had rather done a six weeks' march as troop-horses than been trained for a race. The sports, which were continued the following day, were of the usual kind witnessed at such meetings, and were varied by the falls and other mishaps which are the lot of amateur jockeys. It was rather dangerous, I found, to walk about the streets of Kandy, owing to the ferocity of the native dogs. The moment they see a European they rush at his heels, and he has to be always on his guard to protect himself against their attacks. The streets are picturesque, and the town, which is in the centre of the coffee district, is much frequented by the planters.

Returning to Colombo, I started by the British India Steam Navigation Company's ship "Burmah," which was the first steamer that passed the place bound for India, and, after calling at Point de Galle, arrived, all well, off Negapatam on the 26th February. Passing from the steamer to a cargo-boat, we reached the beach through a surf which deluged all on board with spray. I thence walked to the "bungalow," which was kept by a Frenchman, and having had a tub and a good dinner, went out for a stroll through the town, but found that beyond the streets, which were very pretty and shaded by trees on each side, there was very little to see. I had not yet got accustomed to the presence of lizards in my bed-room. Here I had to share it with several, white and black, and felt so uncomfortable in consequence that next morning I even dispensed with my tub, so anxious was I to be free of their company. I accordingly took my departure from Negapatam and, after a tiresome journey by railway, arrived at Madras.

Chapter V.

MADRAS—BOMBAY TO BUNDER ABBAS.

THE intercourse with India is now so great that there are few Englishmen who are not more or less familiar, either from experience gained by actual travel or from reading, with the leading features of its chief cities. I shall not, therefore, attempt any description either of Madras or Bombay, but will simply state that during my stay at both places I made preparations for my journey through Persia. At Madras the hottest months in the year are May and June; the coolest January and February. I was so far fortunate in arriving there at the so-called cool season, which, however, was so disagreeably hot that only the thinnest and lightest of clothing could be worn. Resolved to return home *via* Persia and Russia, and knowing that I should have, therefore, a good deal of riding to do, I began my preparations by buying a bridle and saddle, a double-barrel gun and a brace of Colt's revolvers, with plenty of ammunition. When I had made all my purchases it occurred to me that I had also better procure some credentials as to my nationality, and the fact of my travelling for pleasure, as I was sure to want such a document or passport on getting into Russia. Calling on a merchant whose acquaintance I had made on the voyage from Southampton, he received me in a very hospitable manner, and gave me permission to use his name as a reference or in any other manner it might be of service to me. I then proceeded to the Fort, and after waiting some time, saw the gentleman in charge of the Passport Department, and obtained from him the necessary papers. As it was getting late, and my friend had invited me to dinner, I made all haste back to my bungalow or hotel, and, with the assistance of a native servant, was soon dressed and ready. The natives make very good servants, but require to be watched. The climate also renders it necessary that more should be employed than would be required in an English home, and their duties are as clearly defined as are those of the *employés* of a Government department. A well-appointed Indian household consists of the following, the pay including board wages, as no servant, except the Amah, or nurse, is fed and clothed in an Indian establishment :— A butler (called " Dobash " at Madras, " Khansaman " at Calcutta), who has the entire management of the household. He superintends the culinary department, checks the bazaar accounts, and hires and discharges servants. His pay is from 20 to 35 rupees, or from £2 to £3 10s. per month, and every under-servant in the establishment has also to allow him one rupee, or 2s. per month, out of his wages. An under-butler (" Khetmutgar," " Bhaiee " at Calcutta, and " boy " at Bombay), who waits at table; pay, from 8 to 9 rupees per month. A valet or body-servant (" Khidmatgar"), whose duty it is to bring coffee or tea early in the morning, to brush clothes and boots and arrange the things to go to the tailor and washerwoman ; pay, 10 rupees per month. A cook (" Bawareh ") who has to go to the bazaar at 5 A.M. and make the necessary purchases; pay, from 5 to 20 rupees per month. Indian " Bawarehs " have very few cooking utensils, yet they manage better than our English cooks at home. An under-cook, who gets next to nothing in the way of wages, and who has often to pay the head " Bawareh" for learning his art. The chief " Hamall " (" bearer" at Calcutta). He takes charge of the entire bungalow, and is responsible for everything which is lost or stolen; pay, 8 rupees per month. The "under-Hamall," or punkah-puller; pay, 7 rupees per month. The "Darban," or doorkeeper; pay, 8 rupees per month. The sweeper (" Mihtar," or " Metranee);" pay, 2 rupees per month. A water-carrier (" Chusti " at Bombay, " Puckally " at Calcutta and Madras), who fills the baths, &c.; pay, 8 to 20 rupees per month. A washerman (" Dhobee"). He comes once a week and conveys the linen to the " Dhobee-tanks," or public wash-houses. A coachman (" Gariwan," " Ghareewalla " at Bombay). The faster he drives the better, and his pay is from 15 to 25 rupees per month. A groom (" Sais " or " Ghorawallah"), who sleeps near his horse, and every horse has a separate groom; pay, 10 to 20 rupees per month. A messenger, or Sepoy, who wears a belt across his shoulders, on which is affixed a silver plate with his master's name and address on it; pay, about 15 rupees per month. An "Ayah" or lady's-maid; pay, 14 to 20 rupees per month. The "Amah," or wet-nurse, who is fed and clothed in the house. A gardener, or "Mali;" pay, 8 rupees per month; and a palanquin-bearer—an office which is going out of use.

Having spent some very agreeable days at Madras, I started by the railway for Bombay, and had in the same compartment with me a very amusing travelling companion. I judged him to be a great native "swell," from his large retinue of servants, who at every halt came to wait upon him and receive his orders. He had a round, flat face, wore a snow-white turban, and was dressed in all other respects like the upper class Indians. He spoke English, and after passing the usual salutation of "How do you do?" relapsed into silence for some time. Later on he spread his bed out on the seat opposite me. Most Orientals take their beds, which are rolled up in a bundle and occupy little room, with them when travelling. After he had arranged his couch to his satisfaction, he slipped off his shoes and sat cross-legged on it. Having asked me in the most polite manner whether I objected to his chewing betel, and been told that I did not, he took from a box by his side two silver vessels containing betel and a preparation used with it, and proceeded to enjoy himself. Meanwhile, I undid my rug and lay down to sleep. When he saw me undoing the rug, he chewed slower and attentively eyed me; but when I lay down and prepared for rest he ceased masticating altogether, and asked me whether that was my bed. I replied in the affirmative. His eyes almost started from his head with surprise, which was doubled when I told him that all my luggage was in the leather box at my feet. He was curious to know how I managed to travel with so little; but when I assured him that it was too much, and that I should send some of it home, he evidently thought that I was humbugging him, and thereupon turned in and slumbered. The journey was terribly hot and tedious, the distance between Madras and Bombay being about 700 miles, and the pace of the train very slow. In the belief that it was the terminal station, I got out at Byculla, a suburb of Bombay, but discovering my mistake, and not liking the hotel at the place, I drove on to the town and took up my quarters at Watson's Esplanade Hotel, than which, as I afterwards learned, I could not have made a better selection. The greater part of its framework, which is of iron, was brought from England; and though not so large as the Langham or Charing Cross Hotel, it is still of considerable size, and is capable of dining several hundred visitors. Learning that the next steamer for the Persian Gulf would not start for some days, I continued the preparations which I had commenced at Madras. I inquired about a tent at a Parsee's store, but he asked a fabulous price for it. Fortunately, on going back to the hotel, I spoke to a gentleman about my plans, and asked his opinion upon them. He told me that it was the custom all over the East to sleep at the caravanseries, and that a tent would therefore be of little use. I took his advice very readily, and thought no further about the tent.

Sending my portmanteau home, and otherwise reducing my luggage to the lowest possible point, I took passage on board the British India Steam Navigation Company's steamer " Ethiopia," of about 1,000 tons burden. She was almost new, and being free from cockroaches, was very comfortable. I was again fortunate in having a state room to myself. Leaving Bombay on the 15th of March at 4 P.M., we arrived, all well, at Kurrachee on the 17th. The harbour looked very snug, but it struck me that vessels of any great tonnage could not enter it with safety. The Telegraph Company's ship, which is used for surveying the coasts, repairing cables, &c., and one of her Majesty's gun-boats, which in these parts are called " Bombay marines," lay at anchor in it. Before going ashore I went on board the gun-boat with a friend and spent an hour or so in pleasant conversation with her officers. As she had been on the Gulf station for some time, I thought I might get some information from them as to the mode of travelling in Persia. They could merely tell me, however, that from what they had seen the people were a semi-barbarous race, and travelled chiefly on horseback and on camels. My fellow-passenger who had introduced me, and who was himself an officer on board a " Bombay marine," advised me to change my mind and not to undertake the journey; but I would not be dissuaded from it. Some of the officers accompanied us to the "Ethiopia," and once on board her brandy and soda and "Trichinopolies" (a kind of cigar much smoked by Europeans throughout India) became in much request. Kurrachee is hot and sandy, and the swamp between it and the harbour swarms with snakes, pelicans, and many descriptions of sea-birds. The next morning we resumed our voyage and arrived off Guadur, on the Beloochistan coast, on the night of the 21st of March. It was so dark that nothing could be seen. One of the boats was lowered and took the mails ashore, and on its return we steamed away from the place, which is one of the Indo-European telegraph stations; and reached Muscat, on the coast of Arabia, on the 23rd of March at 11 A.M. The harbour is small, allowing only four or five moderate-sized vessels to swing in it at the same time, and we did not perceive it until we were quite close to the land. It is surrounded by very high cliffs, and is therefore well sheltered in certain winds. At our arrival the wind was in the wrong quarter. A long, heavy swell rolled into the harbour in consequence, and dashed with great violence against the rocks. There is a small fort built of stone and wood on each side of the entrance. I was told that a vessel once came into the harbour for hostile purposes, and that the noise and reverberation of her guns were so great owing to the confined space, that parts of the forts were shaken down. They are now in ruins. The town is situated at the end of the cove. A few Europeans, who belong principally to the Indo-European Telegraph Company, live there; but for my part, I thought penal servitude at Portland would be preferable to a residence in it, though in my subsequent travels I found places much more desolate and much less inviting than Muscat. The town itself is very dirty. The hills about it have a dry, arid aspect, like those at Aden, and the land is quite barren for some distance from the sea. Dates and wheat are the chief products of the place, and its exports are drugs, ostrich feathers, horses and ivory.

On leaving, our decks were a little less crowded than they had been up from Bombay, but there were still on board a great many natives, who always go as deck passengers.

One old woman and her daughter had secured the hatch on which to make their beds, and had completely encircled it with carpets and jars filled with all kinds of fruits and sweetmeats, which Orientals always take with them when travelling, water alone being supplied to them by the ship. They were accompanied by an old man, who proved the most attentive and vigilant of escorts. He was always on his legs fiddling about with one thing or another; and as his charges smoked continually he had plenty to do in filling their pipes, a duty which required some art efficiently to perform. Another of our passengers, but of a very different kind, also attracted my attention. I noticed him for the first time as I was one evening leaning over the poop rail. He was of rather rough appearance, and evidently a European, and was sitting on a chest smoking an Arabian pipe, which was so short as almost to burn his nose. In the course of conversation with him he gave me a brief history of his life. A tailor by trade, and with a great love for travel, he left his native country, Moldavia, early in life, and had spent many years in the East, paying his way from place to place by working at his craft. He could speak English, German, French, and several Oriental languages, with a little Persian. He was then bound for Bagdad; but hearing of my intention to visit Persia, offered to become my servant, an offer which for obvious and prudential reasons I declined. Our saloon passengers included one or two telegraph clerks, a gunboat officer or "Bombay marine," and a French merchant, who caused us many a laugh. He had a capital appetite. At dinner his cries for "rosbif" would gladden the heart of any Briton. On one occasion his black servant, who always stood behind his chair, brought him lamb instead of "rosbif." Terrible was his rage, and awful would have been the punishment of the trembling servitor if the chief officer, who was a jolly old Scotchman, had not interfered in his behalf. When not eating he was talking, and when not talking he was eating. Between him and the gunboat officer many a scene occurred which relieved the tedium of the voyage. The marine's *forte* was contradiction. Be the subject of conversation what it might, it made no difference to him. The less he appeared to know about it, the more persistently did he contradict; and it was only necessary for the Frenchman to say that the colour of a particular thing was white, to provoke from the marine an assertion that it was black.

On Monday, the 25th of March, we arrived at Bunder Abbas; and here it was that I fortunately heard of Hagee Ahmed, a Bushire Arab, who accompanied me as my servant through Persia. Every one bore testimony to his excellent qualities as a servant, but admitted at the same time that he required to be kept in order. They advised me, however, to engage him, as he could speak Persian and enough of English to act as interpreter for me, and was also a good cook, having been for some time employed in the Indian navy in that capacity. His appearance impressed me. So far as size and strength went, he looked his character, and I was willing to give him credit for the good and useful qualities with which his friends endowed him. He readily agreed to go with me; but I postponed entering into arrangements with him until we should reach Bushire.

Whilst we lay at Bunder Abbas a few of the passengers and myself, with one of the ship's officers, went ashore; and as we walked through the place a strange spectacle came under our observation. Leaning against a wall was a man in an almost perfectly nude state. His head rested on his arms, and behind him sat a little boy gently rubbing the calves of his legs, which were stretched to their greatest tension, with rough grass. When we drew nearer we noticed that he was covered with blood, the rough " shampooing " to which he was being subjected having frayed and torn away the skin at different parts of the legs. We were puzzled for an explanation of such strange conduct, but ultimately learned that at Bunder Abbas such " shampooing " is considered a specific cure for rheumatism. I do not know what the College of Physicians may think of it, but for myself I should regard the remedy as worse than the disease.

After strolling about for some time, we determined on calling on the Sheikh. His house was surrounded by a wall of mud and stone, about fifteen or sixteen feet high, and the entrance was through a large massive wooden gate, which was guarded by a man armed with a scimitar and matchlock. On our knocking, the warder appeared, and demanded our business. We replied that it was our wish to see the great Sheikh. Upon this he disappeared for some time, and, on coming back, threw the gate open, and led us across a yard paved with stone to a large hall. Passing through this hall, we ascended some stairs to the right, and then entered the reception-room, where the Sheikh was seated on a piece of carpet, with one of his ministers or advisers by his side. The floor of the room, which was not very large, was quite bare. There were several recesses built into the whitewashed wall, for no very evident purpose, and the glassless windows were placed about twelve feet from the floor. The Sheikh wore a beautiful and richly ornamented turban. His coat consisted of a gold-embroidered velvet jacket, which fitted rather tightly to the body, and contrasted with his trousers, which were of ample dimensions. His minister's dress was of a more sober hue. We advanced up the room through a row of black slaves, who salâmed a good deal as we passed. When we drew near, the minister rose, and came forward to greet us. We then, each in turn, went up to the Sheikh, and shook hands with him after the European fashion. This ceremony over, some chairs were brought in for our accommodation. They resembled cottage chairs, appeared to have done a good deal of service, and were apparently kept as curiosities rather than for ornament or use. When seated, conversation began, and was carried on through our interpreter. We told the Sheikh all about the Franco-German war. Only vague rumours of it had reached him, and these, when heightened by his fancy, assumed so ridiculous and laughable a character that we had some difficulty in maintaining our gravity while he detailed them to us. He inquired why we also did not fight. We replied that the quarrel was none of ours—that we did not belong to either of the contending nations. He found some difficulty in comprehending our explanation, and was evidently surprised and disgusted at our exposition of the principle of neutrality. After conversing about a quarter of an hour, coffee was brought in, and served on silver trays, in small cups about the size of egg-cups. It was of a strength and bitterness which I cannot describe, and, after partaking of it, I was very glad and prompt to taste the sweetmeats which were subsequently handed round. We then rose, shook hands once more with our host, walked through the line of bowing slaves to the court-yard, which we re-crossed, and were bowed out through the gate by the Sheikh's major-domo.

That evening, while sitting in the cabin, my friend the marine again endeavoured to dissuade me from my undertaking. The officers of the ship also represented to me its danger, especially at that particular time, and recommended me to accompany them on to Bussorah, which was about twelve hours' steaming beyond Bushire, and thence return to Europe *viâ* Bagdad. I felt grateful for the interest which they took in my welfare, and was moved by their representations; but, on reflection, I determined to adhere to my intention, unless I should find later on that I could not safely and successfully reach the Caspian Sea by the route which I contemplated.

Chapter VI.

BUNDER ABBAS TO BUSHIRE.

LEAVING Bunder Abbas after a short stay, we arrived at Linga on the 26th of March. Here the second officer, the Frenchman, and myself went ashore with the mails, and paid a visit to a pearl merchant, whose home gave no indication of his wealth. After ascending some rickety stairs we entered a room in which we found an old gentleman bearing a family likeness to Mr. Fagin in "Oliver Twist." Seated on a carpet, he had some boxes before him, and was in conversation with one or two dealers who had evidently just finished transacting business with him, as they were tying up bundles of papers. He immediately consented to let us see some of his pearls, but before opening his chests caused sherbet to be handed round to all in the room. I took a glass of it, thinking it would be much the same as that which I had drunk at home, but I was mistaken. It was extremely sweet —so sweet, in fact, as to give it a sickly taste. I swallowed it as I would physic. I could not say what it was made of, but the sherbet in common use is composed of the juice of raisins, honey, violets, and water. After we had all tasted the liquor, the "Kalian," or Persian pipe, was brought in. It consists of a stone bottle about ten inches high by three and a half inches in diameter, with a neck a little stouter than that of an ordinary bottle, and with a second neck projecting from the side. Into this latter the stem used by the smoker is inserted. The stem itself, which is made of wood, with (if of the better sort) a silver mouthpiece, is about two or three feet long, and through it the smoke is inhaled, not merely into the mouth, as with English tobacco, but into the lungs. Into the neck of the bottle another tube, but of much larger dimensions than the stem, is inserted, and on the top of this is placed the pipe-head, which is about eight inches or a foot in height and about two inches in diameter, tapering gradually to about the thickness of the main stem. It is made sometimes of silver and sometimes even of gold. The bowl of one which I sent home was an ostrich egg, covered with a stout net-work of silver on the bottom, to protect it during use. The main stem was handsomely worked, and the head, in which the tobacco is put, was made of silver, of a very pretty pattern, and had silver chains several inches in length suspended from it. Persians of wealth could no doubt show many which would surpass it, but I saw none more unique; and my chagrin may therefore be conceived when, on returning home, I found that only the head had reached those to whom I had forwarded it. It is very agreeable to smoke one of these pipes, especially after a good dinner. It is customary to take only about a dozen whiffs, and then to pass the pipe on to your next neighbour; but before doing so, particularly if your next neighbour be a Persian, you must take care to remove the head from the pipe, draw out the smoke, replace the head, and then pass on the pipe. This is a custom which I never saw once neglected during my travels in Persia. The poorest beggar observes it. There is a great art in preparing the pipe, and I was told that few were able to do it to perfection. Indeed the Shah has servants whose duty it is to fill his pipes. It is their sole occupation, and it is to be presumed that his " pipe-fillers," at least, have attained perfection in the art. The tobacco must be of the best kind. It is generally to be got at Shiraz, about ten marches from the sea-coast, and is bought in the leaf. Placed in a little dish it is crushed until it is pretty firm, when a little water is mixed with it, and it is then allowed to stand for some time. When the pipe is prepared, a few wood embers are placed on the top of the tobacco, which not only light it, but keep it burning—a state which it would be otherwise difficult to maintain, owing to the dampness of the tobacco and the space through which the smoke has to be drawn. Cold water is placed in the bottle. It is sometimes mixed with rose-water, or otherwise scented, and the smoke, thus cooled and perfumed, is inhaled with increased pleasure. The first few whiffs from the pipe are said to cause nausea and head-ache. I cannot, however, vouch for this statement, because my servant always lighted the pipe, and therefore took the first whiffs, enjoying the pleasure or suffering the pain which may accompany them.

After the Kalian had been removed, the merchant opened his boxes and displayed his treasures, of which he took the greatest care, guarding them as if he had but little faith in our honesty. He would not open two boxes at a time. One by one he undid them, and then narrowly watched us while we inspected their contents. Knowing little about such things, I occupied my time in smoking and observing the play of features on the part of our host and my friend the French merchant. The one was elated at the prospect of a profitable sale; the other was rejoiced at having the chance of seeing such a collection of precious stones. He, however, bought none. The firing of a gun from the steamer was the signal for our departure. A second and then a third gun followed, and we made haste for the shore, feeling assured that there was cause for the urgency displayed by those on board the ship. The explanation was obvious when we got to our boat. While with the pearl-dealer the wind had risen, and was now blowing in strong gusts dead upon the shore. We had in consequence to tack, which was dangerous work, as the sea was running high, and after a wet and stormy sail at last reached the ship, and succeeded in getting on board, though with some difficulty. We found the captain in no mild humour at our delay. The shore was a lee one; the wind was rising fast, and we were not surprised when he declared that if we had stayed an hour longer he would have sailed without us.

About 7 A.M. on the 28th I was aroused out of my sleep by the chattering of many voices near my cabin-port, which I had left open during the night, on account of the fineness of the weather. On looking out I saw that it came from the crews of some dozen canoes, and that they were paddling with all their might to keep up with the steamer, which was going only about half-speed. We soon came to an anchor about two miles from the shore, between which and us there were some breakers. Farther in lay Bushire. Situated on a peninsula which is formed by the open sea on one side and the bay which constitutes the harbour on the other, the houses come down to the water's edge, and are built after the Persian fashion—of mud with flat roofs. Viewed from a distance it looks rather picturesque, owing to the number of date and palm trees planted about it; but, on a nearer approach, it assumes an arid and, it is needless to say, dirty appearance. An English ship-of-war and a gun-boat lay not far from us. After breakfast we went on board the latter. By and by a boat from the man-of-war pulled towards us, and was followed by one belonging to the gun-boat. The Frenchman gazed intently through his glasses at both for some time, and then exclaimed, with a delicious *naïveté*, " Vat a difference between ze two boats! Ze royal navy ship's boat looks worth seven of ze ' Bombay marine.' " Our friend and fellow-passenger the marine was silenced; he allowed the remark to pass unchallenged. The Frenchman was for once, but unconsciously, victorious.

On reaching the shore we repaired to the telegraph station, which was close to the place where we landed, and enclosed by a high wall, like all the houses in Persia. I now finally made up my mind to attempt the journey across the desert. I accordingly once more returned to the " Ethiopia," and, having collected my traps, finally left her amidst the hearty cheers and good wishes, which I returned with all my heart, of her passengers and crew. The telegraph superintendent, who had come on with us from Bombay, had generously offered me the hospitality of the station. I readily accepted his invitation, and made his house my home during my stay at Bushire.

Chapter VII.

BUSHIRE.

MY first walk through the streets of Bushire revealed to me the fact that the friends who had represented to me, on board the "Ethiopia," the difficulty and danger which I should certainly experience in attempting to reach the Caspian Sea *viâ* Persia, had not been indulging in idle or fanciful talk. They spoke of a failure of crops having occurred in the country the year before and of the people suffering all the horrors of famine —famine such as can only be witnessed in Eastern lands. I could not realise the idea which the word was intended to convey. Poverty enough I had seen at home. Sensational accounts of alleged deaths from starvation in the midst of plenty I had also occasionally read; but I now witnessed—what I hope I may never again witness—a whole people perishing for want of food. The situation and trade of Bushire saved it in some degree from this extreme of human misery. Still the sights which were to be met with in its streets were so horrible that even now the bare thought of them makes the blood run cold. De Foe could describe them. I can only barely enumerate a few, as illustrating the depth of misery in which the whole of Persia was plunged at the date of which I speak.

Entering the town for the first time, and noting its narrow and dirty streets and dismal-looking houses, I came on a scene which realized the Scriptural story of Dives and Lazarus. A trader with a placid and contented mien was seated behind his stall, on which were exposed for sale dates, bread, and many other articles of human food. It was not, it must be admitted, a tempting display. Myriads of black flies were battening on it, and imparted to fruit and bread their own dark hue. But, then, Lazarus would have been grateful for a crumb from Dives' table; and there sat, or rather lay, Lazarus (for he was too weak to sit) in front of the rich man's stall. Afflicted with a loathsome disease—his torments aggravated by the flies which forsook their daintier repast to gorge upon his sores, he gazed with ravenous eyes on the food for want of which he was perishing. But Dives seemed unconscious of his presence, or had become so accustomed to skeletons that one more or less made no difference to him. He offered Lazarus never a crumb. A little further on three children were huddled together stark naked on a piece of matting. They were so reduced by want that you could count the bones in their little bodies, and their limbs were so wasted that it was painful to look on them. They were of course a prey to black disgusting flies. Flies swarmed about their heads, gnawed at their eyes, filled nose and mouth, and covered their bodies, giving to them a blacker shade than they otherwise would have possessed. Near this sad group lay an infant about four months old. It was mere skin and bone, and so fragile-looking that I feared to touch it. Flies were banqueting on it. We had scarcely passed these sights when a woman who was too weak to stand, and was dragging herself along the ground, endeavoured to stop us. She was nearly half naked, having even parted, for food, with the white cloth which no woman in the East, of any position, fails to put on when going out. Her dark brown skin was drawn tightly over her sharp bones, and her breasts hung like pieces of parchment down to her waist. Others of her sex also famine-stricken I noticed threw them over their shoulders to have them out of their way. Looking up at us with a most pitiful gaze she called "Sahib" in a voice so weak and sad that it was impossible to resist her humble and pathetic appeal. I gave her a "khran" and was repaid with mute thanks. Poor creature! she had not strength to express them, but I am sure she felt them. These sights, which were surpassed by others that I witnessed as I penetrated into the country, caused me to hesitate for some time as to whether I should proceed further with my journey. My host, of whose kindness and hospitality I shall ever entertain a grateful recollection, again urged on me with increasing solicitude its danger, and advised me either to take the route to Bagdad or to wait for the return steamer, and so home by India. I had not however yet realized the situation. An unwillingness also to confess defeat without an effort to carry out my plan likewise influenced me; and so, after long and anxious deliberation, I resolved, come what would, to prosecute the adventure with a resolute and hopeful heart. I therefore at once began the final preparations for it.

The completion of the engagement with Hagee Ahmed claimed my first attention. He agreed to accompany me from Bushire to Teheran, to serve me to the best of his ability, and to enter into a fresh contract if his services should be required beyond Teheran. It was further agreed that his pay should be 20 rupees, or about £2 per month, and these terms having been arranged the agreement was reduced into writing in English and Persian. Hagee immediately entered upon his duties. He proceeded to collect the necessary cooking utensils and such other like matters which we should require on our journey. I had brought my stores of preserved meats, vegetables, &c., in tins from Bombay, and was consequently already supplied with provisions. The rest of my kit, excluding revolvers, saddle, and gun, did not weigh above forty pounds. It included my bed, which consisted of two thick English horse-rugs, water-proof sheet, and a sack in which to put straw to lie on. This, however, I did not use until I had experienced aches and pains from lying on the hard floors of the caravansaries. I also took a hatchet for the purpose of chopping wood, but, owing to the scarcity of that material, had never an opportunity of using it.

On overhauling my stores with the view of making an inventory of them, I found to my surprise and annoyance that I had left my powder, which was in a tin box, with caps, bullet-moulds, &c., on board the "Ethiopia." Passengers are properly not allowed to carry powder below in these steamers. My box was accordingly lashed on deck near the wheel, and was forgotten by me in the hurry and excitement of my departure. The intelligence of my loss was received by my friend and host with great delight, he believing that it would cause me to prolong my stay in Bushire, and share for some time longer the hospitality of his roof. He, however, so far sympathized with me that he agreed to accompany me to the bazaar, where I hoped to be able to obtain a fresh supply. We started for the town for this purpose with our respective servants at our heels, and it was on this visit that we encountered the heart-rending sights to which I have already referred. Such miserable stuff was sold for powder at the bazaar that I purchased none of it. The bazaar itself was very inferior to others which I had seen, but was pervaded by aromatic smells which were not displeasing. Leaving the bazaar we went to a store kept by an Armenian. His collection of goods was of a most miscellaneous kind—a compound of Wardour Street and Petticoat Lane. Ready-made European clothes, old gloves of various shades, ladies' boots of every style, guns, pistols, swords, preserved meats and pickles, and knick-knacks of every description, all thrown together in picturesque confusion, and all covered with the accumulated dust of years. I bought from him a Persian gun, which I sent home with some other things. Only about a quarter of them however reached their destination, and those in a very sorry condition. Powder was also procured from the Armenian, and I had a very primitive bullet-mould made at the bazaar.

My greatest difficulty arose in respect of horses. I examined several, but all of them had such backs that they were quite unfit for travelling. At last I heard of one which belonged to a store-keeper, whose name I shall not attempt to write. I could only with difficulty pronounce it. I found the horse a fine Arab entire, but small, and with only a little Persian blood. All the other horses I had seen were of Persian breed, and I was told that an Arab horse would sell much better than any other up the country. This of course settled the question, the horse itself being free from blemishes. I accordingly purchased him. I afterwards discovered that the story of the superior value of the Arab horse when you come to sell him was the dealer's fancy, for I had to part with mine for a mere nothing. Putting the saddle which I had bought at Madras on him, I mounted and rode outside the walls of the town on to the desert to try his paces. I started well, but the horse stopped and slackened his speed so suddenly that I with difficulty retained my seat, although not unused to riding. I was puzzled to account for his sudden stoppage as I had hardly touched the bridle. On dismounting I readily discovered the cause in the Persian "bit" which he had in his mouth. This bit is a most barbarous contrivance. The bar instead of being a flat piece of iron is a round ring with a rod through the centre. The rod is rather pointed at the top, and when the horse is pulled comes in contact with the roof of his mouth. He is by this means suddenly stopped, and when need be thrown upon his haunches. I returned to the town and changed the Persian for the English bridle I had brought from Madras. The effect was magical. The horse went lively and at the same time so gently that a tiro in the art of riding could manage him. The weather being very warm, and many open wells being scattered over the plain, I did not ride at any very great rate. On getting back to the gate Hagee Ahmed declared that my pace had not been half fast enough. I accordingly allowed him to mount, when he darted off like an arrow, and " dodged " the wells in a way which it was a pleasure to behold. I had heard many people speak of the Persian saddle as enabling any one to ride the most restive horse. Such has not been my experience. One can certainly remain in these saddles if he only holds on by the high pommel in front, but when real riding has to be done anyone not accustomed to them will find them very awkward. They are covered with cloth, and are decorated with gold and silver fringe or other rich material; and though they may not strike an Englishman's eye as serviceable, are certainly picturesque. The stirrups are broad and flat, in shape somewhat like a shovel. I was much struck with the skill displayed by the Persians in mounting their horses. They are in fact adepts in the art. The pack is invariably carried behind the saddle when on the march, and rising in the stirrup they will easily clear this with the right leg, which is carried to a height that would seem ludicrous if the movement were not performed with celerity and grace. The native saddlers also sell powder flasks (made of leather and stamped with devices), and other accessaries to shooting, and large and dangerous-looking knives, fit to cut an ox in two. After some trouble and delay Hagee succeeded in procuring mules, the muleteer being of course named Hassan. The original Hassan, by the way, was the eldest son of Ali and Fatima, daughter of Mahomet, and was born in the third year of the Hegira, A.D. 625. From him all Persians derive the name. The mules were packed to my satisfaction; and at last, after much worry and anxiety, everything was complete for our long and lonely journey across the Desert.

Chapter VIII.

BUSHIRE TO BURAZJOON.

WE took our departure from Bushire on the 1st April. Hagee with the baggage had started in the forenoon, and was to wait for me at the first village, some ten miles outside the town. I left about 4 o'clock in the afternoon when it had become a little cooler. My appearance was calculated to strike terror to the heart of the beholder. My double-barrel gun rested on my holsters, in which were stuck a brace of Colt's revolvers, and at my side hung a large knife. My host and his servant, who was armed with a Persian gun, were to accompany me for some distance beyond the walls, so we all started off together. Once on the plain we put our horses to the gallop, Hagee Bakre, the Persian attendant, firing off his gun and loading it again while at full speed. It was interesting to watch him and observe the way in which he managed his horse by the pressure of his knees, handled his weapon, or lay half-concealed on the side of his saddle. My little Arab horse showed himself quite capable of outstripping the other two, at which I was very glad, knowing the value of speed in case my safety should later on lie in flight. We kept up the pace for about four miles, and then slackened speed in order to look out for some one to guide me to the village. The sun was getting redder every minute, the night would soon be on us, and the village lay ten miles across the morass which stretches to the right and left of Bushire, as you face it from the sea, and is also many miles in breadth. I had heard that even the natives got lost in it, so few were the landmarks and so great was its extent. Possibly it would not be dangerous if it could be traversed in the day-time, but the caravans are obliged to make their marches during the night, owing to the overpowering heat of the sun in the day, and it is therefore difficult to keep always the proper track. We had fortunately not long to wait when a man appeared. On being questioned he professed his knowledge of the whereabouts of the village, and readily undertook to guide me to it for a few "khrans." The sun was now low, and my friend was anxious to get back into the town before it was dark, in order to avoid the danger arising from the numerous wells on his way. He accordingly reined in his horse and repeated the instructions anew for my guide, and then came our leave-taking—the shaking of hands and the oft-repeated good wishes, on his side for a safe and pleasant journey, on mine for kindness and hospitality which was as cheerfully offered as it is gratefully remembered. Another shake of the hand, a wave of the hat, and he and his servant were lost in the distance.

The British political agent resident at Bushire had promised to let me have a native guard. They were to have come up with me about where I now was, so I waited for an hour, but no guard appeared. At last the sun being quite low, and on the point of setting, I gave the signal to my guide, who started off at a kind of jog-trot, half walk, half run, which took him over the ground at about five and a half miles an hour. I had never before seen such a peculiar run. My little Arab soon got into an agreeable amble, which made my seat in the saddle as comfortable as if I had been in an arm-chair. Whilst waiting for the guard my guide had more than once pointed to the sun, in fact, it was only when he had pointed to it a third time that I gave the signal for our start. This anxiety or impatience on his part was not unreasonable, as subsequent events proved. The darkness rapidly increased until I could see only about twenty yards ahead. Our way lay across the morass, and at one moment my horse's fetlocks were deep in mud, and in the next we waded through sheets of shallow water. Now and then we passed heaps of bones, apparently of large animals. By degrees they became more frequent and at last seemed to line the way on each side. All this time my guide kept up his pace, but my wonder at his endurance changed into anxiety when after about four hours' such travelling there appeared no sign of the village. The roll of an approaching thunderstorm added new terrors to the situation. The rain came down in thick drops, the thunder grew louder and louder, and lightning flashes lit up the scene. At the first flash my guide pointed to it with a look of apprehension, and quickened his pace, so that I was now frequently obliged to put my horse to the trot to keep up with him. My anxiety was further increased when I remembered the quantity of steel I had about me. We had just passed a sheet of water, when a terrific flash of lightning darted from the heavens and illuminated the morass for miles around. It revealed no sign of human habitation, but threw a ghostly light on an object, the sight of which chilled my heart. There on the other side of a pool lay the dead body of a victim of famine. It was the first I had seen and I felt stunned at it. To approach it was impossible, because of the foul stench which it emitted. My horse scented it and stood still. I gave him the butt-end of the gun, but he would not move. Then came lightning so vivid and prolonged, followed by such an appalling thunder-clap, that terror-stricken he reared and plunged and I nearly lost control over him. I instantly dismounted, fearing that he would run away with me, in which event possibly my bones would be added to the heaps which were scattered over the sterile plain.

I now walked with the guide, holding the horse by the head. We had not gone much further when the man stopped and looked round, went on again for a few minutes, and again halted, throwing his hands over his head and giving me by other signs to understand that he had lost the way. He was also tired, and had to sit down for some minutes to rest. On rising he resumed his walk, but now slowly, and every now and then shouted out a phrase which sounded like "Beezou!" and which I afterwards learnt meant "Come here!" Another half-hour passed in this way when my ears caught the distant sounds of "tom-toms" and other barbarous instruments of music. The sounds grew louder for a time and then gradually died out, our hopes of reaching a shelter by their means fading with them. My guide was now so fairly exhausted that I would have given him my horse were it not for the obvious fear that he might draw one of the revolvers and so terminate my wretchedness, or, galloping away, leave me to my fate. The storm now reached its height, and the horse became so unmanageable that the Persian had to assist me in holding him. I fired several shots from my gun in the hope that if any one were about he would come to our assistance, but all in vain. The telegraph poles were also fruitlessly searched for, and then I thought of trying back on Bushire, but found that the rain had obliterated our track in the sand, and that this our last hope should also be abandoned. During this time, noticing that the Persian had become so weak that he could no longer call " Beezou!" I took up the cry and continued shouting it, but had no response. I was now seriously alarmed, although the storm had passed away and the stars began to shine. At last, after shouting until I was hoarse, I observed a faint light in the distance and soon a man on horseback came riding towards us. On approaching I noticed that he lowered his long gun into a handier position. I instinctively looked to my own and prepared for the worst. When he drew near my guide spoke to him for some time, after which they both started off at a good round pace, beckoning me to follow them, which I did, although not without some misgivings. We did not go far before a large object came in view, and this I found, to my great relief and delight, was the long-sought-for caravansary. We pounded away at the gate, but no one answered. The Persian on horseback once more struck off and disappeared in the darkness, which was, however, soon dispersed by numerous lights from the inside of the enclosure. A chorus of barks from different points now saluted our ears; further consultation took place between the Persians, and a kind of parley with those inside the enclosure; the gate was suddenly opened, and in a moment we found ourselves in front of a large fire, at whose cheerful blaze five or six dusky figures were warming themselves. For it must be remembered that, although the days are burning hot in Persia, the nights at this time of the year are quite chilly. Closer inspection showed my mules securely picketed, and, summoned by loud and continued shouting, Hagee made his appearance, and admitted me weary but thankful within the shelter of a village hut. The village itself was now in a state of commotion, all its inhabitants running about and imparting to each other the intelligence that the "Feringhee" had arrived.

The meal which Hagee had provided for my dinner now served as my breakfast. After partaking heartily of it, for fatigue and long fasting had sharpened my appetite, I went out to view my quarters. The village, I found, consisted of a number of mud huts scattered over about half an acre of ground, and, like all the Persian villages, was surrounded by a fence made of mud and sticks. Within this enclosure the sheep and goats, which in the daytime browse on the patch of thin rough scrub which grows close to the village, are gathered at night, and are thus protected from savage dogs and beasts, and the still more savage marauder who roams the desert. Each village has its own chief, who administers its simple laws in primitive fashion. The fire which I had noticed on my entrance into the enclosure was still burning. Before it, stretched at full length and fast asleep, lay the wearied companion of my wanderings across the morass. The Persian whom we had met stood close by, leaning on his gun, and chatting to a number of villagers who were grouped at his feet. He was a magnificent specimen of his race—tall, erect, strong, and graceful. His dress, which differed but little from that worn by all the poorer classes in Persia, consisted of a hat or skull-cap of dark-coloured felt and a coat of the same material with enormous sleeves, which were thrown over his shoulders. Beneath the coat he wore a long blue shirt, but his feet and legs were quite bare. His size and apparent strength alone would have impressed me. I was, however, equally struck with the contrast which his appearance presented in another respect to that of his fellow-countrymen of the same grade. I lately saw in one of the illustrated newspapers a drawing of starved and emaciated beings taken from a slave-ship at Zanzibar. Such, as a rule, did the poorer classes in Persia look at the time of which I speak. They were mere skin and bone, spiritless and feeble. He, on the contrary, appeared well fed and muscular. This fact, combined with his numerous weapons and the hour at which we met him alone on the morass, caused me to think that he was one of those lawless bands against whom the traders have to guard by travelling in caravans. Those who travel on horseback seldom join the caravans, because of the greater speed at which they can move. My adventure of the previous night was evidently the subject of conversation among the group, and I observed that Hagee, who had joined it, was listening with deep attention to the tall Persian, who heightened the effect of his story by gesture and action. Several women and girls were hovering about, criticizing the appearance of the "Feringhee." I was flattered by their attention, though truth compels me to state, in defiance of gallantry, that they were not the most lovely of their sex. Having looked to the mules and my horse, who neighed when I approached him, which proved that he knew me, I lay down to rest for the few hours which had to elapse before commencing the day's march. I had scarcely done so when a yellow lizard made its appearance, and darted into a hole in the wall near my face. I had now become used to these creatures; so sticking a piece of flannel into the hole, and thus effectually imprisoning my unwelcome visitor for the night, I gave myself up to slumber.

It seemed but a very short time—it might have been counted by minutes, I thought—before Hagee aroused me. Refreshed by a cup of coffee, which, with a biscuit, constituted my first breakfast, we were soon ready to start. The morning was just breaking, and revealed the dreary waste which in every direction stretched as far as the eye could reach. Quicker and quicker the sun rose, until it was soon blazing high in the heavens, when the heat became excessive. I had long ceased to wear a vest. The coat had now also to be discarded, but even this afforded only temporary relief. The solar helmet was, however, comfortable, and I had fortunately on my feet close-fitting shoes made of canvas, with rags and other soft material for their thick soles. They are called "gievas," and are specially adapted for mountain walking and riding during the heat of the day. With a blazing sun over-head, black leather boots would have been unbearable. About noon the mid-day halt was called. A little hole in the sand was dug, a few lighted sticks were placed in it, and the coffee was soon made. A tin of preserved meat was also opened and eaten. The repast over, we were once more in the saddle and on the march. Soon we came up with a caravan, consisting of a long string of camels, wearily wending its way across the desert. The pace of the camels is very slow, the Persians reckoning that they take double the time of horses, or even more, in performing the same journey. A caravansary lay about six miles to our left. A long caravan was entering it, but it looked so inhospitable and uninviting, although some palm trees grew about it, that we did not care to seek its shelter. We accordingly continued on our way. After crossing a large plain, our track lay through a line of date-trees, which, however, afforded no shade, so far were they apart. It was my first experience of travelling in the desert. I was completely exhausted by fatigue and heat, and was rejoiced when we came in sight of the walls of Burazjoon.

Chapter IX.

BURAZJOON TO SHIRAZ.

AS we approached the town, Hagee told me that there was an Armenian at the station. I could not at first make out what he meant, but, on further questioning him, learnt that Burazjoon was one of the testing stations of the Indo-European Telegraph Company, and that it was in charge of an Armenian. I resolved to put up there instead of at the caravansary. We accordingly directed our steps towards the station, which, like the other places of the kind I had previously seen, was protected by a high mud wall. Entering through the open gate into the enclosure, and thence into the room in which the telegraph instruments were kept, I found the Armenian sitting at a table in his shirt, with a kind of white apron twisted round his waist, and his feet stuck into loose Persian shoes. I told him that I was travelling through the country, and that I wished to put up at the station. He spoke English, and readily acceded to my request. It must, however, be remembered that the hospitality accorded to the traveller in Persia, under the circumstances in which I became a self-invited guest at the station, extends barely to the shelter of its roof. Hagee prepared my dinner, which I directed should be on a liberal scale, with a view to the entertainment of my host, who agreed to share the repast with me. He brought with him, however, rice, chicken, and curry of his own, of which, fortunately, as it subsequently turned out, I did not partake. We sat down and ate in silence for some time, when a second Armenian came in and took his place at the board. He spoke no English. Taciturn like his friend, he partook of the rice and curry, but scarcely was the dinner over, when both were seized with illness, which assumed the form of violent vomiting. I knew not to what cause to attribute it. They declared that poison had been placed in the food, but by whom or for what reason they could not tell. Happily they soon recovered. The circumstance was an unpleasant one, and I could not for some days get rid of the disagreeable thoughts which it suggested.

Like myself, the second Armenian was also on the march, and bound for Shiraz. Being alone, he asked to be allowed to join my party for the sake of the protection it would afford him. I readily assented, and then went out on the plain with my gun in search of game, but could find nothing bigger than a sparrow. In my absence, a large party of Persians arrived at the station. One of them seemed a man of some consequence, and with him I was invited to converse. I told him about the Franco-German war, and was met by the inquiry addressed to me by the Sheikh at Bunder-Abbas, if I also had fought. The explanation on this point brought our talk for the time to an end. Turning, then, to the Armenian in charge of the station, the Persian addressed him first in a loud tone, then in whispers, which became more and more mysterious. My curiosity was thoroughly excited. At length, after long confabulation and many glances at me, the Armenian approached; and when I expected some such demand as "Feringhee, your money or your life!" came out the inquiry, "Have you any brandy?" I was as much taken aback by the query as if the more terrible demand had been addressed to me. I confessed that I had a little, which I had brought with me in case of illness. This seemed to damp them considerably, and they were gloomily taking their departure when I asked them whether they would not taste the Feringhee's "water." The invitation acted on them like a charm. Their faces beamed, and they chattered away like so many magpies. Hagee brought a bottle of the coveted liquor. I poured a little into one of my iron cups, and handed it to the "swell," who declined to take it until I had tasted it myself. Holding it in his hand for a little while, and smiling with glee, he smelt the liquor, and then made a gulp at it, as if he would swallow the whole contents of the cup. But what a change! No sooner did he put his lips to it than he pulled a wry face, comical in its misery, and passed the cup in silence on to his followers, who tasted it in like manner and with like effect. Surprised at his not relishing the spirit after the anxiety manifested to obtain it, I asked for an explanation, and was told that some of his acquaintances who professed to have drunk it had boasted to him of its delicious quality and rare virtue, and that he had in consequence conceived a longing for it. He added that he believed they had never tasted it, and that their talk must have been brag. On his departure, the Armenian gave me his history, which was a career of violence and crime. It may be thus summed up—he was the "headman" of the village or town in which we were, and he had obtained his position by the murder of his brother.

Next morning before sunrise we were again on the march. It being still cool, we moved at a good pace, the stars, which were shining brightly, enabling the cattle to pick their way over the stones with which the path was strewn. It is quite wonderful, the manner in which Persian horses and mules, the mules especially, travel over such ground. They will pass along the bed of a stream filled with boulders with rarely a slip, and will make good their footing on the steepest mountain path. We soon came up with a caravan, which was going the same way, and had some difficulty in heading it, owing to its great length. Once in front we rapidly drew away from it and the jangle of its bells, of which each mule carries at least one. Further on the air became tainted with the smell of naphtha, which came from wells filled with a black-looking liquid. I got off my horse to inspect them, and on a nearer approach found the smell excessive but not disagreeable. The sides of the wells were impregnated with the liquid, which resembled fluid in a congealed state. I spent some time in examining them, and was thinking how glad I should be to have a few of them on the property at home, when my reverie was interrupted by Hagee calling out, "Sahib, come here quickly! I see something." Putting my foot into my stirrup to be able to get a better view, I saw a couple of deer about 500 yards off. I immediately drew the bullets from my gun, reloaded with swan shot, and began to scramble on my hands and knees towards the deer. But scarcely had I got 200 yards when a crawling thing, like a lizard, over a foot in length, came actually running at me. I was so astonished that I jumped up and, in the flush of the moment, blazed away at it. The deer were startled at the report. I gave them the second barrel, but the distance was too great for execution. This was the only game I met with from the Persian Gulf to the Caspian. I returned with a sorrowing heart to my party, and we resumed our journey.

We had not proceeded above a mile from the naphtha wells when we came up with a body of Persians. The chief among them was smoking the "kalian," which looked a very unwieldy affair when used on horseback. After exchanging a few words with Hagee, he came forward and offered me the pipe, which I accepted, taking care, after I had had a few whiffs, to remove the head and blow the accumulated smoke from the stem and bowl before returning it. Knowing the difficulty of keeping the pipe alight, I wondered where he could have got the live charcoal, which is kept on the top of the tobacco. When, however, his retinue passed, I noticed that one of them, whose horse was rather heavily laden, had suspended from the pack at the back of his saddle a small grate made of wire, and that it contained fire, which burned brightly owing to the current of air caused by the motion of the horse. From this the live charcoal was taken, and food was also cooked over it while the party was on the march. Indeed, they had got no great distance from us when the servant drew from the grate what possibly was an appetising morsel, and rode forward with it to his master, who ate it with evident relish. The contrivance seemed well adapted for desert travelling, and suggested the idea whether the hordes, who swept down upon Europe from these wastes in ages past, carried with them a commissariat arranged upon an equally simple plan. During this and the previous march we saw many starving people, but as yet only a few dead bodies, which were being gnawed by ravenous dogs and vultures.

Our next halting-place was the caravansary of Kumah Taktah, as well as I can recollect. Having no idea that I should ever commit the history of my tour to print, I made few notes, save of the dates of my arrival at and departure from the chief places on my route. Its incidents, however, are still so vividly impressed on my memory that I have had no difficulty in recalling them, but the names of some of the smaller villages and caravansaries have got confused in my mind and I am not sure whether I always call them by the correct name. It was the first caravansary proper at which we had put up, and I was therefore curious to observe what kind of place it was. In describing it I describe all the other caravansaries of the country. They differ only in size. The one in which we now were was of the larger kind. It was built of mud and a species of brick, and was in the form of a square. The yard inside was capable of containing a large number of camels, mules, and horses, with their packs. In the centre of it brickwork in the form of a cube was built, but for what purpose it was intended, I never could make out. The most natural supposition was that its object was to aid in the loading and unloading of the animals forming the caravan, yet I never saw it used for that purpose. Along the sides of the building numerous recesses were built, about three feet from the ground, and of tolerable dimensions. As the caravans arrive, each party occupies one of these recesses, and here the travellers rest safe from prowling beast and lawless bandit. The caravansaries are, as it were, common property. No toll is charged for their use, but sometimes a native, half-mendicant, half-villager, takes up his abode at the gate, and receives a small gratuity for keeping the recesses clean, and providing firewood. At least, he is supposed to occupy himself in the performance of this duty. But sleep is his chief business, and to this he gives his whole mind. A well is sometimes sunk within the yard of the buildings. Water is always to be found in their neighbourhood, and their situation along the desert routes are well known to the caravans. Indeed, without them, travelling in the interior of Persia would be impossible.

When we arrived, the place was crowded with travellers of every class, and resounded with the neighing of horses and the shrill cry of mules and camels. Only one recess was vacant. It was so dirty that I did not care to occupy it, and so endeavoured to effect an exchange with a neighbouring party, which I succeeded in doing, by some persuasion and a little gentle force. Actual force was, of course, out of the question, for if injury be done in any quarrel the matter becomes a blood feud, and life is taken for vengeance. When we were as comfortably lodged as could be expected under the circumstances Hagee brought the evening meal. Though

I had felt very hungry before, I now lost all appetite, and could not touch what was offered me. Soon after I became quite sick and very dizzy and feverish, and was disturbed all night by wild fantastic dreams, which took their shape from the place and scene in which I was placed. Hagee soon divined my illness, which was occasioned by exposure to the sun. I had in the latter part of the march omitted the use of my solar helmet, and was now paying the penalty of my neglect. Hagee at last took me out into the cool night air, which revived me a little. In the morning the fever had passed away, but then came dysentery, which I attributed to a too free use of water. I did not, however, cease drinking water during the attack, which lasted ten or eleven days; and although I afterwards never hesitated to slake my thirst, no matter what kind the well or stream might be, I never had a recurrence of the complaint. The different caravans were early astir, preparing their scanty morning meal. The glowing fires gave a cheerful aspect to the place, which was now all bustle and excitement. Some were packing the animals, others were endeavouring to get them in order when loaded, and all were frantically gesticulating and shouting; the mules and camels swelling the chorus until the din became deafening. But of all the noises of which it was composed the song of the muleteers was the most terrible. It is in truth a wild howl, and is frequently kept up by them all the night long. They may have found pleasure in it; I did not.

It was still dark when my party were ready to start. Giving the gate-keeper a gratuity, in consideration of the fire-wood with which he had provided us, we left the caravansary, and followed a track which led over large stones and slippery rocks. We were now for a time about to leave the plain and cross one of the many mountain ranges which intersect the country. As the morning advanced we could trace our path for a long distance a-head. It lay up the side of a precipice, and looked so steep and dangerous, that I should have doubted the possibility of climbing it, if I had not caught sight of a string of mules which were making the descent. It was exceedingly narrow. At some places the path was strewn with huge boulders, at others the packs of the mules touched on the one side the rock, and on the other hung over a yawning abyss. It cost us some labour to get to the summit of the pass in the day, other caravans which blocked the way having to be "shunted," and tired mules, falling under their packs, dragged up the ascent. Many famine-stricken wretches were also passed on the way, and dead bodies became more numerous. I had now to some degree overcome the feeling of horror with which the sight of them at first filled me. I had not, however, reached the point of callousness to which the scenes which we encountered between Shiraz and Teheran brought me; and my reflections were not of the happiest as I lay awake that night at the caravansary, listening to the dismal song of two Persians who were vocal until the morning.

We were again on the march before daybreak. Weariness, if not disgust, now possessed me. The sunrise was no doubt beautiful, the sunsets even more so; the great luminary of day sinking below the far distant line of the desert horizon with the effulgence with which he dips into the sea. It was also a pleasure to note the effects produced by mirage. They almost invariably assumed the appearance of lakes, and while exciting hope, which was never to be realized in fruition, afflicted the traveller, exhausted by excessive heat and parched with thirst, with the sufferings of Tantalus. Still, the drawbacks to the pleasure which, under other circumstances than those in which Persia was now placed, might have been derived from the journey, were great. Not only had we to witness human misery of a character and extent beyond our power to relieve, but we had often to make double marches—in some instances as many as forty miles a day—owing to the difficulty of getting straw to feed our cattle, or of providing fresh ones.

Our next halt was at Kazcroon, which proved to be another of the testing stations of the Telegraph Company, and also in charge of an Armenian. Here we put up and stayed for a day, in order to give the mules rest. Here, too, I had the satisfaction of seeing the starving people fed by English charity. The morning after our arrival, a crowd of emaciated natives poured into the yard of the station. Some sat on their heels, some propped themselves up against the wall, others lay wearily at full length on the ground. They numbered in all—men, women, and children—a couple of hundred. They were all in rags or more than half naked, and the effluvia from them was so fetid, that although standing on the top of the station, about twelve or fourteen yards off, I could scarcely bear it. They were of all ages; but their suffering seemed to have told most on the children. The girls looked like hags, the boys like aged dwarfs. Two or three Persian " gholams "—men who, when the telegraphic communication is interrupted, go down the line until they discover the place at fault—stood at the gate, in order that the very poor and starving might alone enter. I could not make out what test they applied to discriminate between the famished and half-famished, but I noticed that they rejected very miserable-looking women who supplicated for admittance. Another " gholam " assisted the Armenian in distributing the dates, the form in which the relief was given. When the dates were brought in, every device was resorted to in order to obtain a double supply; and the crowd sometimes became so wild that the trays on which the fruit was placed were upset, and what might in truth be termed a life and death fight was fought over it. The distribution over, the unhappy beings got back as they best could to their hovels to pine and suffer, sustained only by the hope of a future dole at the station.

On that evening Hagee came to me with a face of ominous length. He told me that the muleteers had heard that some lions had been seen prowling about in the neighbourhood of the path which we should have to traverse the next day, and that they were unwilling to proceed farther on the journey. I ridiculed the story, and succeeded with much difficulty, but only for the time, in dispelling their fears. Next morning they reluctantly packed the mules, making every possible delay in the operation. Our agreement was that I should give them sixty "khrans" before starting (which I did), and forty more on arriving at Shiraz within ten days. I reminded them of it. The prospect of gain, combined with fresh argument and remonstrance, had its effect, and we at last, long after sunrise, marched from the station. No lions happily crossed our path, and no dangers had to be encountered save those which are ordinarily incidental to travelling through a difficult and semi-barbarous country. At length, on the 10th of April, on rounding the span of a chain of mountains which we had been traversing for the day, we beheld in the far distance Shiraz.

Chapter X.

SHIRAZ.

SEEN from the point at which we first sighted it, Shiraz, which we reached within the time specified in the agreement with the muleteers (ten days from Bushire), presented in nearly all respects the appearance of the other Persian towns which I had already seen. It was, however, much larger, and was studded with towers and minarets. I could also note that it had many outlying gardens. As we approached the town our caravan had to wind its way through many of these gardens, and through the openings or subterranean passages by which water is conveyed to them. They contained the only patches of verdure and green trees which I had seen for some time, and were most refreshing to the eye. When within a mile of the walls a horseman came towards us at full gallop, and handed me a note. It was an invitation, the news of our arrival having already reached the town, from the superintendent of the telegraph station, to put up at his place. After the "gholam," for such the messenger was, had delivered the note, he placed himself at the head of our party and led the way. As we rode through the gate much the same sights as those which were to be seen at Bushire presented themselves. We were assailed by a swarm of beggars who had to be kept back by a free use of the "chappar" whip. They looked the very picture of misery, and their importunity was maddening. The street through which we first passed was almost dark, being covered overhead, and was not more than ten feet wide. The slush was quite a foot deep. The mules sank in it, and the smell would have been intolerable were it not for the strong aromatic odours which pervaded the place. A few hundred yards on, a camel came lumbering towards us and blocked up the way. It was the first difficulty of the kind which I had to encounter, and I knew not how to grapple with it. Hagee shouted out to strike the brute on the head with my whip. This done it came to a stand-still, viciously opening and closing its mouth the while. The driver at last came up, and backed it with much difficulty into a recess or opening provided for such emergencies, and so allowed us to pass. After threading our way through many such streets and alleys we reached the door leading into the Compound of the superintendent's residence. He welcomed me in the most cordial manner, and, after we had smoked and drank some Shiraz wine, led me to my room to rest, for it was now past two o'clock in the afternoon, and I had been marching since three in the morning.

The sight of a camp-bedstead in the corner of the room excited in me the hope of sound and refreshing slumber. It was a luxury to which I had been a stranger for some time, and I rejoiced at the prospect of a change from the hard floors of the caravansary. My hopes were soon dispelled. The bed was so soft and hot and the room so close that I could not sleep. I was therefore rejoiced when summoned to dinner, the more especially as I had not partaken of anything during the day beyond a cup of coffee. On entering the dining-room I was much surprised to find a lady sitting near the window. She proved to be my host's wife, and received me courteously. The accent with which the "How do you do?" was spoken struck me as very peculiar, but the words were so distinctly pronounced that I concluded she understood English, and so became profuse in my compliments, which, judging by her smiling face, I was happy to think were rather well-chosen. My confusion was great when, on the entrance of her husband, I learned that she was ignorant of the English language, and could only repeat a few of our ordinary phrases of courtesy. She was of average height, young, and good-looking, and as fair as an English woman. After dinner the "kalian" was brought in and presented to the hostess, who was an Armenian. It was then passed on to her husband and myself, and by its aid and some good Shiraz wine, which tastes something like sherry, seasoned with pleasant conversation, I spent a most agreeable evening—the first, indeed, in which I had enjoyed lady's society since leaving Bombay.

Learning that mules and horses were scarce,

I directed Hagee to look out at once for such as we should want. He professed all zeal in the matter and departed on his mission, returning, however, without either mule or horse, and much the worse for liquor. Next morning, penitent and sober, he again started off on the quest, and brought back a few sorry-looking animals, with large ulcers on their withers. It was impossible that they could do our work, so I at once rejected them. On his return, after a further search, he informed me that no serviceable horses were for sale, and that we should have to travel "chappar," (as the Persians pronounce the word,) which means that we should merely hire horses, ride them to the next halting place, there procure fresh ones, and so on throughout the journey. I could see no objection to the arrangement, and directed him to make preparations for our departure.

As the muleteers were to return to Bushire in a few days, I thought I would avail myself of the opportunity to send some tobacco down with them to the coast, to be forwarded with other purchases from Bushire to England. I accordingly ordered my horse and started off for the bazaar, Hagee following on foot.

The bazaars which I had hitherto seen were open like an English market-place. This was covered, presenting the appearance of a large arcade, and was about a quarter of a mile in length, but narrow in proportion. The streets leading to it were, as usual, dirty beyond description, and so full of ruts, that if my horse had not been very sure-footed, he would certainly have brought me to the ground. The place was crowded with traders and purchasers. Beggars flocked round the recesses or shops where food was sold, and fought like hungry dogs for the spoils of the dust-heaps. Here, in what might fairly be called a centre of trade, famine was as apparent as in the scattered villages through which I had passed. Entering the bazaar and pushing our way through the throng we came to a recess where tobacco was sold. The merchant who sat within it was composedly smoking his "kalian." We informed him that we wanted 200 lbs. of best tobacco. No way surprised at the extent of the order, and scarcely deigning to look at us, he quietly threw us packages of the different kinds which he had for sale. These were duly tasted, and a selection made; but when the tobacco reached England—I forwarded 180 lbs.—it was seized by the Custom-house officers at Southampton, on the ground, as I have been informed, that sugar and salt were mixed with it—the importation of tobacco so manufactured being prohibited.

The most novel, if not the most interesting, sight which I witnessed at the bazaar was the coinage of Persian money. There was no mystery about the process—the Mint was open to all. The coin of most value in the country is the "toman," and is always used in calculation when large sums of money have to be denoted. It is a gold coin, but I did not see many in circulation. The coin next in value is the "khran." It is composed of alloyed silver, and is the current coin of the kingdom. Then comes the "penebad" of base metal, and lowest of all, the "shais." The "shais" has an extensive circulation, but the "khran" and "half-khran" are most in use. The "toman" is equal to ten "khrans," the "khran" to two "penebads," and the "penebad" to ten "shais;" and as compared with English money the value of the "toman" is about $9s.\ 0\tfrac{5}{8}d.$, and of the "khran" $10\tfrac{1}{2}d$. The "khran" was the coin which I saw minted.

The metal was prepared in long bars, which were placed on a kind of anvil. A piece of the requisite weight and thickness was cut off, and upon this the die was fixed and struck with a hammer, the process being so negligently conducted that sometimes only the edge of the coin was impressed. The operation could be seen by all who chose to stop and observe it; and, judging by the crowd who surrounded the Mint (for such I suppose I must call it), and the general appearance of the place, there must have been a brisk demand for the coins. Shiraz is the Sheffield of Persia. It has many manufactures, but it is chiefly noted for its swordblades, which are of the finest temper. It has likewise a reputation for soap, but the use of the article I should say is very limited in the country itself. In 1852 the town was visited by an appalling calamity in the shape of an earthquake. Nearly 12,000 people were destroyed by it, and the memory of the event is still recalled with terror. As I could not safely count upon being able to procure fodder for my horse on the journey to Ispahan, I here parted with him, with regret which was not diminished by the amount of the sum for which he sold. It was a mere trifle.

In the evening, at dinner, my host informed me that bad news which might concern me had reached him. It was to the effect that the doctor attached to the telegraph station had been attacked, whilst on his way to Ispahan, by the savage tribe of the Backtiary, who stripped him of his clothes, and robbed him of everything which he had about him, and then dragged him up into the mountains, from which he escaped during a dispute between the robbers about the division of their plunder. My friend represented that, under these circumstances, it would be foolhardy for me to advance farther into the country, and advised me to wait at any rate for a few days, until we saw how matters stood. This, however, I was reluctant to do. The weather was becoming hotter every day, and I felt that each day's delay would add to the fatigue of the journey. After dinner he again reverted to the subject, expressing the fear that I was too young and inexperienced to encounter the risks of the enterprise I had undertaken. My reply was, that my success so far emboldened me to pursue it; and after this, seeing that my resolution was not to be shaken, he helped me in every way he could to procure horses and all else that I wanted. In fact, from one and all of the Europeans whom I met in Persia I received nothing but kindness. They were the most generous of people; but it was impossible to be oppressed by their hospitality, which could only be repaid by thanks, such was the frankness and cordiality with which it was proffered.

Later on in the evening we were startled by the report of cannon, which evidently came from the large square of the town. As we had nothing else to do, I proposed to go out and ascertain the cause of the firing. My host accordingly called a "ferrashe," or servant, and directed him to get a lantern, which is made of paper, like the Chinese lanterns sold in the toy-shops, is about two feet in height, and collapses into a circular tin frame when not in use. Without a lantern it would not be safe to pass along the streets after dark, for not only are they full of dirt and ruts, but in some of them wells are also sunk. In many instances the sides of these wells are crumbling in, and they are all completely unguarded. Having further provided ourselves with two stout sticks, we made our way as best we could to the Telegraph Station, which was situated in the Square. The place was illuminated with torches, the bearers forming a line along its sides, and was crowded with people. In the centre a body of Persian soldiers, in varied and motley uniforms, were drawn up, and were engaged in loading and firing some half-dozen pieces of cannon. The mode in which they performed the duty was so alarming that I was heartily thankful we were out of the line of fire. No sooner had the rammer driven home the charge than out would come the rod with a jerk, giving the man with the fuze a violent blow, and occasionally rolling him over. I had never seen so many Orientals gathered together before; and I therefore gazed long on the scene, which, notwithstanding much squalor and other drawbacks, was very interesting and picturesque. In the centre of the Square was a high pole, which served as a gibbet for malefactors, and a means of inflicting torture and minor punishments on other offenders. The torture practised was, as I was told, often of the most cruel kind—so cruel that I fear to indicate it, lest it should be deemed a traveller's story. The firing, we were informed, was in celebration of the birthday of the Shah's wife—I suppose I must call her the "Queen of Queens," the Shah, as the representative of the ancient Persian monarchy, claiming the title of "King of Kings;" and after witnessing the loyal demonstration we returned to our home, following the crowds that now filled the streets.

Next day there was an Armenian wedding, to which my host was invited. He asked me to accompany him, which I most gladly did. The house, the residence of the bride's father, was in the centre of the usual Compound, but was shaded by some fine trees. Many shrubs were also planted about it, and a few rows of flowers, which, with some ornamental water, gave it a pretty, if not elegant, appearance. My surprise was great when, on entering, the travelling Armenian whom I had met at Burazjoon, and whom I allowed to join my caravan, came forward and greeted me with much cordiality. He was the last person I should have expected to meet as a guest at such a gathering, for he looked poor, and the surroundings showed that we were now at the house of a wealthy and influential man. However, there he was, and we both rejoiced at our meeting. My friend and myself had unfortunately arrived too late for the ceremony. The company were now assembled at the wedding breakfast, and were making merry over sweetmeats and sherbet. The bride, who was easily recognized by a rich, though gaudy, dress, sat on a terrace in front of the house. Around her were gathered several women, young and old, who were all uncovered and enjoying themselves; at least they laughed much and whispered more. I could not distinguish the bridegroom, and had little opportunity to criticise the bride and bridesmaids, for my Armenian fellow-traveller so overwhelmed me with dainties that I had serious thoughts of seeking safety in flight. Having eaten as much sweets as would have made any one but a seasoned school-boy ill, we took our departure, not waiting for the termination of the feast.

Hagee's love for drink and the other pleasures which are to be found in a large town, made him in no hurry to leave Shiraz. Promises of amendment he made in abundance, but the resolution formed in the morning was forgotten in the evening, and so time passed. I had resolved to journey with a caravan to Ispahan, but the difficulty of purchasing either mules or horses was so great, owing to the state of the country, that I had to change my plans and arrange to travel "chappar." I accordingly despatched Hagee to the "chappar kaneh," which is a kind of livery stable, to ascertain if there were any horses there for hire. He came back with the intelligence that there were three, which were quite sufficient for our purposes. I afterwards managed to travel with only two (they became scarcer as we proceeded), but to do this I had to cut down my kit to almost the clothes I stood in. Shortly afterwards, a man led up the animals. They appeared nothing but skin and bone. It was, however, a case of "Hobson's choice," so I agreed to take them, and promised the fellow ten "khrans" extra if he were there on the following morning before sunrise. Stimulated by the hope of reward, he was punctual to the appointment. The horses were packed, leave was taken of my generous host and hostess, and on the 14th of April I took my departure from Shiraz.

Chapter XI.

SHIRAZ TO ISPAHAN.

BEFORE leaving Shiraz the intelligence as to the plunder and narrow escape from death of the doctor of the Telegraph Company's staff by desert robbers had been confirmed. There were reports also of other acts of violence by them. Allowing for every exaggeration, these rumours filled my mind with serious thoughts. I began to fear that I had under-estimated the dangers of the journey, and my fears were in no way lessened by the descriptions which were given to me of the tribes amongst whom I should now have to travel. There are several of these tribes scattered over Persia. Most of them are marauders by habit and nature, but some live by their flocks and the manufacture of certain descriptions of carpets. At the best, however, their industry is very fitful. The Illiats come under this head. They are a numerous body, and consist of several small tribes called "Teeras," which are ruled over by petty chiefs of their own, all, however, being subject to one superior chief. During the winter months they come down to the villages in the plain. Here they remain until the weather becomes warm, and then return to their mountain homes with their flocks, for they are a pastoral people and live in tents. The cloth of which the tents are made is black, and when first manufactured can be seen through; but it contracts after a few showers of rain, and then becomes pretty much waterproof. The chiefs live in white tents, which, in addition to the respect the colour indicates, also denote where the head of the tribe is to be found. Some such mark is, indeed, necessary, for the tribes seldom stay long in any one place, and their tents are always scattered over the plain. In the north the shape of the tents differs slightly from those in the south, and the sides consist of mats instead of cloth. Goats are their chief stock. They make cheese from the milk, but their main industry is the manufacture of the celebrated Persian carpets. I was very anxious to see how the carpets were made, but could not get the opportunity to gratify my curiosity. The tribe is of Turkish origin. I do not know, however, whether they still retain the use of the Turkish language. They are very hardy and inured to great fatigue, and are capable of hardship in any temperature, hot or cold, wet or dry. The Backtiary are a very different class of people. They are considered the most numerous and powerful of all the Persian tribes, and are also distinguished by their lawlessness. The branch or sub-tribe who inhabit the plains of Hamadon, and are known as the Karagoozelli, or "Black-eyed," are esteemed the most warlike of all. They also excel in horsemanship, which they continually practise; but I question whether they would exhibit like skill if, instead of the native saddle, they had to use one of our "pig-skins." Under such circumstances, I think they would often measure their length on the ground. The Turcomans are also an important tribe. Like the Illiats, they are a pastoral people, which obliges them to range over immense tracts of country to procure food for their flocks; and like the Illiats also, and in the same fitful manner, they manufacture carpets. Their "Ordous," or camps, acknowledge a chief, who governs them, not by a fixed law, but just as he thinks fit. Rough justice roughly administered it must be, but doubtless more acceptable to a rude people than the most perfect code. Every man able to bear arms is only too anxious to do so in order to protect himself and family and his property, which consists of horses, camels, buffaloes, asses, goats, and sheep, of which the tribe, as a whole, possess immense flocks. Their horses are splendid animals, those that I saw ranged from 15—3 to 17 hands high, and their best points can be seen whilst walking, a thing which cannot be said of most of our horses at home. The men of the tribe are in the saddle from morning until night; they bear an unenviable reputation, but though Mussulmans, and practising all the rites of Mohammedanism, are in no way as fanatical as their sedentary co-religionists of the East.

Before leaving Bushire, as well as at Shiraz, I had heard, as I have said, numerous tales of the fierce and almost savage nature of these wanderers of the desert. I did not believe all that I was told, but now that I was about to test its truth, and perhaps suffer for my temerity, I grew anxious and had a troubled and feverish sleep during the night previous to my start for Ispahan. It seemed as if only a few minutes could have passed when Hagee appeared at my bedside and aroused me with, "Time to get up, Sahib; very late; sun will soon rise." Rubbing still sleepy eyes, I jumped out of bed, for I had now become an adept at turning out at any hour and on the shortest notice, and inquired if the horses had arrived. I was glad, though surprised, to hear that they had, so I hastily dressed, got my feet into the "gievas," reloaded my revolvers and descended into the compound. The owner of the horses was there, and, pointing to the quarter in which the sun would soon appear, held out his hand with a broad grin for the extra ten "khrans" which I had promised him. Prudence, gained by my dealings so far with the poorer class of Persians, dictated caution in the matter. I therefore had the horses first packed, and when I had mounted, and not until then, handed over the expected gratuity. All our preparations being now completed, we left the compound.

The thoughts which had oppressed me over night were still present to my mind. They were now dispelled by the appearance of Hagee, who took the lead of the party. Nothing more comical could be seen in a pantomime. He looked a Hudibras and Don Quixote rolled into one. Mounted on a poor animal whose bones were starting through its skin, he had on his feet dirty white "gievas" that had seen much service. His legs were covered with enormous trousers or knickerbockers, the calf of the leg being protected by wonderful and elaborate gaiters, made of yellow leather with red patches here and there, and further embellished by a lot of coloured strings hanging from their tops. Over his shirt he had a jacket of brown-red cloth, which was sadly faded and otherwise the worse for wear before we reached Teheran. It was trimmed with fur, which seemed a rather odd style of ornament in such a climate. Somehow or other, however, the fellow never seemed to suffer from the heat, although his performances in wielding his "chappar whip" would have secured for him a prize at any of our athletic sports. His head-gear was the great feature in his costume. Its basis was the ordinary Persian cap of felt. Round this was twisted his turban, which he well knew how to arrange to advantage, and which was of a rich and tasteful pattern. The edge of the turban was decorated with strings of coloured silk about three or four inches long, which usually dangled over his shoulders. Above these came my solar helmet, which he had put on the wrong way, and all were surmounted by a large, soft, felt hat, which I should want when we reached the civilized world. Hagee himself seemed rather proud of his appearance, and the wonderful structure which he carried on his head, so far from exciting laughter or ridicule in the Persians who saw it, was regarded by them with admiration and envy. On a devout old "Hagee," with a snow-white turban, whom we passed, it had a religious effect; for no sooner did his eyes rest upon it than he averted his gaze and looked devoutly in the direction of Mecca. To me its sight brought back good humour and buoyant spirits, and the journey was resumed with hope and confidence.

A Persian was mounted on the third horse. He was to accompany us to the halting-place, and was to bring back the animals if they were worth the trouble. Mine was the best of the three as regarded condition, but a little hair off the near knee, combined with a suspicious-looking straight shoulder, made me doubt whether I had not got the worst. The pace at which Hagee led the way through the narrow and tortuous streets of the town was startling. Away he went at full gallop, now avoiding a gaping hole by a bare few inches, now skirting a treacherous well, and, still at full speed, turning the most abrupt corners, to the imminent risk of man and horse. My heart was in my mouth during this part of the ride. We were going in Indian file, he was leading, and it was impossible to stop him. The pace was kept up until we reached the town gate, through which we bolted like so many North American Indians, and vanished in a cloud of dust. The way in which the horses went surprised me. Miserably fed and overworked, they had still some fire left in them. We accordingly continued our gallop, but at a less furious rate, and in good time reached the caravansary at which we intended to halt. Great, however, was my concern on discovering that Hagee and myself had outstripped the Persian. The curry and rice were in the pack carried by his horse, and our plight would be sad indeed if they were lost or damaged. After anxiously waiting for him for about half an hour, he made his appearance. The dust on the horse's head and knees sufficiently indicated the cause of the delay. The poor brute had fallen. The Persian was now walking behind it, and was administering to it the most brutal chastisement. My blood boiled at the sight, and I had raised my arm to let him feel, hot and heavy, my "chappar whip," when Hagee suddenly seized me and reminded me of the consequences that might ensue from such an indulgence of my anger. Even with those consequences before my eyes, I felt it difficult to restrain my indignation, so wanton and cruel was the conduct of the fellow. We took the load from his horse and placed it on mine. He did not like the change, and tried to prevent it. This was too much to bear. Enraged already by his conduct, irritated by the delay, and fuming under the rays of a scorching sun, whose heat was intensified by reflection from the burning sands, I rode up to him and gave him a smart cut with my whip across his back. This had the desired effect. Sulky, but not submissive, he no longer resisted. The re-packing finished, Hagee and myself departed from the caravansary, leaving the Persian to follow us across the plain as he best could, or return to Shiraz if he thought proper.

The march from Bushire across the mountains to Shiraz had been hot—very hot. The heat, however, then experienced was nothing to that which we had now to endure. The desert waste, sandy and sterile, stretched away for miles in every direction. The track we had to follow was marked by telegraph poles, which formed an endless chain, and added to the scene its weariest feature. Oh, how depressing it was to see them stretching away into the far distance, and marking the long miles which had to be traversed before jaded traveller and horse could rest! They were offensive to the eye. They disturbed the solitude of the desert, which is its great charm, and were too numerous to excite the train of thought which a solitary gibbet in the waste, like that in the Square at Shiraz, would arouse. In the end I viewed them with hate, and I include them among the evil sights of Persia. Part of this day's march was by the side of a lake. The track, however, lay chiefly across the barren plain, on which no trace of caravansary or other human habitation could be descried. The day was waning, when, on coming to the top of a little rise or mound, I saw the village for which we were bound, about a mile and a half off. Gladdened by the sight, and congratulating myself on having almost terminated the march, without coming to grief with my horse by reason of the bad formation of his shoulders, I was on the point of quickening his pace, when, without the least warning, down he came with his head between his legs. Getting from under him as I best could, and fortunately unhurt, I found on examination that both his knees had been broken, and that they were now badly grazed. The village, however, was not far off, so I again mounted and caught Hagee before he reached it. As we did so, his turn arrived. His horse "came a cropper," but horse and rider escaped injury, though the ground on which they fell was hard and uneven. The chappar khaneh was within a hundred yards, and thither we led our horses without any further mishap.

On inquiring for fresh horses, the chappar khaneh keeper replied that there were only two in the place, and that they had just completed a long journey. Their appearance in the stable verified the statement. They were covered with dust and looked very tired. Mules were also sought for, but in vain. This being the first chappar khaneh at which we had put up, I felt some interest in its arrangements. Up from Bushire we had come caravan, which, particularly in the conveyance of merchandize, means travelling at a walking pace, or at best an amble, which was my case. "Chappar," on the contrary, is the fastest mode of locomotion known in Persia; and if the traveller be a tolerable horseman and capable of enduring fatigue, and relays of horses can easily be procured, as they may be in prosperous times, it is wonderful what a great distance can be covered in ten or twelve days. In this way one hundred miles may be accomplished in the day; but the great feat is to keep it up for ten or more days.

There are few men who can do this; and these few are to be found among either the Persians, Tartars, or Turkish couriers, who, so to say, live in the saddle, and can, it is said, even sleep on horseback. An Englishman whom I once met told me that whilst travelling in the Caucasus he had to ride 400 miles in four days, and that he did it; but that the exertion was followed by a violent fever which prostrated him for weeks. In Persia there is not a town or village which has not its record of some wonderful feat in hard riding. Such feats could, of course, only be performed by relays of fresh horses at certain distances; and these are to be procured at the chappar khanehs, which, as I have already mentioned, are a kind of livery stables. Like the caravansaries, they are built on the same plan. They are in the form of a square. The yard is reached by a door, in passing which the horses have to lift their legs high in order to avoid the stones to which the door is fastened; and around it are the stables, which are generally capable of holding from twelve to twenty animals. The larger chappar khanehs can hold still more. The mangers are very primitive, and the stables themselves in summer time are oppressively close. There is a small room, about nine or ten feet square, over the entrance. Beneath this room is a sort of hall, with a room on each side, and these are used by travellers, chiefly in the winter time, when the smaller apartment is full. The upper room in the establishment at which we had now halted had outside of it a small balcony looking on to the plain. Here I stretched my carpet; and after partaking of some food, lay down to enjoy a pipe and the view of some mountains which rose far away on the horizon. Close by a few Persians were engaged in irrigating a patch of land which looked almost as parched and thirsty as the arid sands around it. The water for the purpose was drawn from a well in leather buckets to the required height by means of oxen, which ran down a slight incline, and when they reached the bottom the contents of the vessels were tilted into the appointed channel.

The sun was now on the point of setting. Large masses of dark clouds were gathering in the sky, and drops of heavy rain gave warning of the coming downpour. I had, in consequence, my bed of carpet and waterproofs prepared in the little room; and this done, I went down to the entrance of the building, where I found Hagee seated at a fire made of the scrub which grows on the plains, and forms almost the total sustenance of camels in Persia. He was chattering away, surrounded by a number of attentive listeners, and our travels were evidently the subject of his gossip. The "kalian" was, of course, being rapidly passed from mouth to mouth. The conversation fell to a whisper at my appearance, and ceased altogether when I pulled out my pipe, intending to learn something from them, through Hagee, as to the state of their part of the country. They intently watched my movements. They were clearly puzzled at the simplicity of my meerschaum; but when I took out my tobacco-pouch and began to fill it, and Hagee explained to them its merits, their wonder passed into admiration. No definite information, however, could be gathered from them to interest or enlighten a traveller. All they could say was that no one had passed the village for several days, and that the way was dangerous. On cross-questioning Hagee, however, I found that they had been telling him a lot of stupid tales, all fabrications, about outrages and murders. Happily he was not a man easily daunted, and I had on many an occasion cause to be thankful that I had engaged him, and not a Persian, for my servant; for I observed that those of the poorer class gave ready credence to every rumour; and I had reason to think that when impressed by such stories as those told to Hagee I should have had difficulty in keeping them to their contracts, and inducing them to face the dangers of the journey. I had lain down to sleep when I heard the main door open and a horseman come in. It was the Persian whom we had left behind us early on the march.

Chapter XII.

SHIRAZ TO ISPAHAN.

(Continued.)

NEXT morning we were again in the saddle, and away before sunrise. Towards the end of the march, we were to come within nine miles or so of Persepolis. This was something to look forward to, and might prove even worth the risk of an encounter with marauders. My dress now consisted of only an ordinary tourist's shirt, a pair of trousers, and " gievas." So hot was it that I had to keep the shirt loose at the throat to catch every current of air, but the relief afforded by this was more in the seeming than in the reality. I still preserve a vivid recollection of those marches—the blaze of the sun, the blinding glare of the sands, the suffocating heat, the panting horses—to ride which was a penance in itself. How the

Persians were able to bear up against it, never showing fatigue or weariness, I was at a loss to understand. Day after day will they ride across the desert, and sit as erect in the saddle at the end of the journey as when they began it. Still more, they are always gay and lively. Fits of silence do occasionally seize them, but seldom. As a rule they are fond of talking, and their language sounded agreeable to my ears. They are very variable as to temper. I have often seen them on the point of fighting, and a few minutes afterwards laughing together as if they were fast friends and nothing had occurred to disturb the good feeling between them. The quarrel, however, is not forgotten. The memory of it is long treasured, and if the opportunity should offer, vengeance for the wrong or insult is surely taken. "Padre S-Ag" (son of a dog) is their common expression of contempt. It is habitually used by those who are well off to their inferiors; but their vocabulary of abuse is not confined to it, for when enraged they give vent to their anger in expressions and epithets which one would not care to see in print.

It was my intention, if time allowed it, to

visit the ruins of Persepolis. It was yet early in the day when we came in sight of it, and I was about to branch off from the main track, when Hagee stopped and desired me to look ahead. On doing so I observed a body of horsemen, about ten in number, emerge from behind the ruins. Several people on foot could also be discerned loitering about the place. Hagee expressed his willingness to accompany me if I were bent upon the visit, but urged me to forego it, because of the risk which it necessarily involved. His reasoning impressed me. Persians were not likely to be at the ruins for any good purpose, and, on the other hand, if the party were the escort of a European, attracted to the spot for the purpose of exploration, we should have heard of his arrival at the chappar khaneh. Prudence therefore bade me be content with all that I could see from the point at which we stood of the remains of the once famed city. It was several miles away from us, but we could, notwithstanding, clearly descry the ruins of numerous buildings which seemed to have been erected on large platforms, and also many lofty pillars rising above the plain.

The sight of them whetted my curiosity; but to indulge it was now out of the question. We therefore held on our way, passing, at some distance from Persepolis, what appeared to be the ruins of another town. We at last arrived at Moorgaut, which was built by Cyrus, the founder of the ancient Persian monarchy. According to Plutarch, it could boast of a magnificent temple to the "Goddess of War," and it contained also the tomb of Cyrus. The place is now in ruins. Even the memory of its glories has passed away. This day's march was the longest and the most trying which we had yet made. It extended to seventy miles; but I had become so accustomed to the saddle, and so anxious to get away from the famine-stricken land, that I should have still held on if fresh horses could have been obtained. Our track was now regularly marked by dead bodies, and beggars and starving people followed us from every village crying for food. During the night two of our horses gave up the ghost. Only one was left, and it was at death's door. We had therefore to spend a day in rest. In the evening some horses arrived at the chappar khaneh and these I at once secured.

Next morning I was awoke early by Hagee, and after a cup of coffee, we were both again in the saddle, and away. Our path now lay over a dangerous mountain pass, which proved almost fatal to Hagee. The path was only a few feet wide, and at one point the ascent had to be made up a steep rock, which shelved off to a ledge about a yard or two broad. Knowing the animals to be at least sure-footed, I gave my horse an extra cut with my whip, and went up the rock with a rush, gaining the summit in safety. Looking back, I saw that Hagee was about to do the same. I shouted to him to dismount and walk up, as he was so much heavier than myself, and his horse exhausted. He either did not hear me, or did not heed my advice. He rushed at the rock, but half way up his horse lost its footing, rolled over and dragged Hagee on to the narrow ledge, below which there was a clear fall of fifty feet. Both horse and rider were stunned, and stuck on the ledge. I instantly jumped off and ran to Hagee's aid. He, however, quickly recovered himself, but all his efforts to raise his horse were unsuccessful. He then commenced beating the poor brute after the fashion of the Persian on a previous march, but I gave him to understand that as I had served the Persian so I should serve him, and he desisted. It was evident that the horse was so weak that he could not rise by any exertion of his own. I accordingly clambered up to my own horse, undid a long piece of rope which was fastened to my saddle, and fastening one end to my horse and the other to the fallen animal, succeeded in raising him, and helped him up the ascent. The place was so difficult and intricate that it seemed just the spot for a surprise. I had scarcely communicated my thought to Hagee, when we were startled by the sound of voices and approaching footsteps. Hagee grew anxious. I shared his anxiety, and looked to my arms, hoping that all would be well, but prepared for consequences. We continued to ascend, and on rounding a huge boulder rock encountered six Persians, all armed with long guns. Retreat was impossible; we therefore advanced with apparent confidence and unconcern, and after exchanging a few words with them, passed on without molestation. They may have been honest men, but their looks belied their character, and their loitering at such a place was quite sufficient to raise a grave suspicion as to their intentions. It was Hagee's opinion that we escaped attack because of the arms we carried, and our evident readiness to use them, and also because of our packs, which were so small as to hold out the hope of only poor plunder. It was also likely, he added, that they were waiting for some rich Armenian merchants who were expected to pass that way, and who would furnish them with more booty than we could do. Be that as it may, the fate of the Doctor, the friend of my host at Shiraz, was present to my mind, and I had fears that I should figure with him in the catalogue of victims to Persian rapacity and lawlessness. I was heartily rejoiced when we had left the group behind, but still kept my pistols ready for use.

On the morrow our road lay at first through a succession of narrow valleys watered by brooks. We then began to ascend again the mountains, and reached an elevation where patches of snow could be seen in the clefts of the rocks. These marches tested our endurance to the utmost; but they were relieved by the mountain scenery, which, though not so grand or beautiful as that of Switzerland or the Tyrol, was bold and varied. Here also, as we had been cautioned, we had to look out for marauders. Our attention was consequently on the alert. Eye and ear were occupied, and the miles were not marked and counted off as so much ground passed over, as was the case when traversing the desert. On the third day we reached the boundary line which separates Iral from Tarsistan; and some hours afterwards the village of Yezidecost could be seen far off across the plain. When little more than half a mile distant, as I thought, I noticed of a sudden that a deep gully, about two miles in length and about a quarter of a mile broad, lay before us, and that we should have to skirt it before reaching the village, which stood on a conical rock on the other side, and reminded me much of the old castles on the Rhine. This was a disappointment, for I was anxious for the halt, not only on my own account, but also for the tired horses. Fresh horses were not to be had at the chappar khaneh. This had long been the rule. I therefore, after partaking of some food, occupied myself in an examination of the town, which was not without interest. Built on a rock, it was a natural fortress, and could be cut off from the surrounding country by means of a drawbridge. Needless to say it was very squalid. Differing, however, from the other Persian towns through which we had passed, balconies projected over the doors and windows of the houses, and from these there hung in festoons every description of tattered garment and dirty rags. My survey was soon completed; so, returning to the khaneh, I went on to the roof, and spent my time agreeably in watching the numerous flocks of goats which were being driven from the plain into the compounds built to shelter and protect them at night.

The villagers all assembled to witness our departure on the morrow. Their "head-man" was also present. When we came to where he was standing, we stopped and saluted him. He at once began to tell us of the dangers of the road, and advised us to return the way we had come, saying that if we proceeded we should surely meet with misfortune. I pointed to my pistols. He gave me to understand that they would be of no use; and with that we parted. It must be admitted that the prospects of a successful march were not great. The horses were the poorest I had yet seen. They could barely walk. Their backs were in a terrible state, and the sores on their withers had assumed the form of ulcers. Shortly after starting Hagee's horse came down. We could not raise it. We accordingly directed a Persian on his way to the village to see the khaneh keeper, and order him to send on the third horse which he had in his stables. An hour elapsed, when a man appeared with the spare horse. The load of the fallen beast (it was only a few pounds) was shifted to him, and we again started. A second mile passed, and down came the animal which I was riding. Like its companion, it instantly commenced to beat its head against the ground, but was too weak to rise. Placing its load on our remaining horse, we started on foot across the plain under a fierce and burning sun. Slow and difficult as our pace was, the horse could scarcely keep up with us. It became apparent very soon that he could not hold out until we reached the next caravansary, and there was no other course open to us but to return to Yezidecost, which we reluctantly did.

There was a wild rush of people across the drawbridge as we again approached the town. Rumour was already rife amongst them. The belief was that we had been attacked and robbed, barely escaping with our lives, and taht the prophecies of the chief had been literally fulfilled. Their disappointment was great when the real cause of our return was ascertained. In a moment there was a revulsion of feeling, and while in the morning we were regarded with respect, we were now received with gibes and jeers. In the East, above all other parts of the world, it may be truly said, that "nothing succeeds like success." So long as you are prosperous you are honoured; let reverse of fortune come, and you are despised. I had now to witness and suffer from this fickleness. Hitherto, as a rule, I had carried with me the sympathy and good wishes of the villagers; now I was the object of contempt. Conscious of this, Hagee and I were astir early next morning, but not so early as to avoid the flattering attention to which we had been subjected the previous afternoon. Our caravan, also, was not of a character to excite admiration. Mounted on two diminutive donkeys (horses were not to be had), followed by a third laden with our packs and in charge of a Persian, we slowly crossed the drawbridge amid the grins of a mocking crowd, and yet more slowly crossed the plain. Happy was I when free from their observation, and when we could bury our shame in the desert. But another feeling soon possessed me. What if marauders should now appear? The thought was unpleasant, and I was glad when about midday we encountered a detachment of Persian soldiers on the march to Yezidecost. If uniform mean similarity of dress, uniform they had not. So many men, so many costumes. Their guns also were of many different patterns. When we came up with them they were halted and squatted around small shrub fires; eating, smoking, and chatting. Some had horses, some mules and asses, others camels to carry their baggage. The heads of the camels were decked out with different coloured wools, and suspended from their necks were numerous bells of metal and tin, with tongues made of iron, wood or stone. When in motion the discord was horrible. As my donkey driver had been rather refractory, it occurred to me that this was a capital opportunity to reform his manners. I accordingly inquired, through Hagee, for the officer in command—he proved to be a general—in order to represent to him the man's disobedience. The general and his staff, who were soldier-like men, admirably dressed, and mounted on magnificent horses, drew up as we approached, and listened to Hagee with the utmost solemnity as he told my story and my complaint—to wit, that I was a European travelling through the country, and that my donkey driver would not make his animals go fast enough. Hagee concluded his short speech in my name with a prayer for redress. Think of an appeal to the commandant of Woolwich against the donkey boys who frequent the common—their bad language, their extortion, and, above all, the pace of their animals! A wave of his mighty hand by the little man (the general was small) before Hagee had well concluded the statement of my case, and the disobedient driver was seized by a dozen soldiers. What was intended in a measure as a joke became now so serious that I was terribly frightened, and repented of what I had done. The man looked as if he expected to have his throat cut, and hope of reprieve there was none, for the general and his staff were away scouring the plain on their fleet horses. The detachment had also resumed its march, and there remained but the executioners, the culprit, Hagee and myself. Happily a sound drubbing was the only punishment inflicted, and though I regretted it, I could not deny its salutary effect. Our pace was excellent for the remainder of the day. This incident, more than any other of my experiences, made me feel that I was travelling in the East. Had the Caliph of Bagdad, or any of the other personages mentioned in the "Arabian Nights," ridden up and asked to join my party, I should not, I think, have been surprised at it. It was the East of the Sultans, Caliphs, Grand Viziers, and Cadis. "Padre S-Ag! He will not drive fast enough. Justice, mighty Caliph, justice! The bastinado — quick. Be warned, remarked the Cadi who superintended the operation, and loiter not again. Ever after no faster driver was known in Ispahan." I was, indeed, in the East, and such was the story of "Hassan the Swift," told me by the merchant just before he knocked the eye out of the Geni's beloved son with the date stone.

This day's march lasted ten hours. The marches which followed it were also severe, and at length we reached a caravansary and chappar khaneh, two days' march to the south of Ispahan. It was late when we arrived. We halted at the caravansary, which was silent and desolate. We rode on to the chappar khaneh. Here the door was gone, having been used possibly for firewood, and the yard was covered with water two inches deep. How it came there I could not conceive, for the ground around was as dry as sand. A faint gust of wind as we entered brought with it the smells of a charnel-house. On looking round I noticed a woman lying on her face. She was dead and perfectly naked, the few garments which she was accustomed to wear having been taken by some other poor creature starving in the chilly nights. Out of the sockets of her eyes and mouth a black and noisome fluid was oozing, and the side of her face and breast was gnawed away. Two famished-looking men and a woman were seated a few yards off glaring at the body with wolfish eyes. A horrible suspicion seized me. Could famine have driven them to this horrible repast? I would not believe, and yet I could not doubt it, so hungry and ravenous were their looks. Passing them, and stepping over two more dead bodies, I came to the stable on the right side of the yard. I entered it, and after waiting until my eyes had become accustomed to the darkness, discovered on the one side the dead body of a man, and on the other side, close to the wall, a woman and a child. The woman was dead, the child just breathed. I hastened with it into the air, hoping that life might still be preserved in it. It was too late. A faint gasp, a mere sigh, and it also passed away. I took it back and placed it with its mother. The corpses in the yard, owing to exposure to the rays of the sun, were swollen to the size of small barrels, and their skins were drawn tight and blistered. The body of the woman whose flesh was gnawed away had not yet reached this stage. She was not long dead, and lay in the shade. I directed Hagee to tell the only living beings in the place to come out and follow us. The woman alone did so. The men did not seem to understand him, and remained still glaring at the corpse. I went away intending to bring them some bread. On emerging from the khaneh some ten or twelve other starving beings, among them a negro, surrounded us and called in heartrending voices for food.

Hagee told them they would get it if they kept back for a time, but still the piteous cry was continued. We passed on, and found at the entrance to the caravansary a dealer who had some bread and other food for sale. A gun and pistols were within arm's reach of him. With these he protected his treasures, surrounded by the dying and the dead, and looked unmoved on the skeletons who besought from him a crust. It seemed to me that only in a monster could such insensibility to human suffering be found as he exhibited. I bought all that he had to sell, and divided it amongst the crowd of miserable wretches who had followed me. Some devoured it like wild beasts, others could hardly swallow it. Three were lying on the ground unable to rise. I put bread in their mouths, but they could not eat it. A fourth was lying on his back snoring. This I afterwards noticed was a marked symptom in famine cases. When it came death was close at hand. We tried to rouse him, but in vain, and so carried what remained of the bread to the two men in the khaneh.

Every minute's delay at such a place was an agony. We therefore went on with the same horses, no food being procurable for them, or fresh horses to be obtained, but had not journeyed far when one of them dropped dead. His load was put on the back of the other horse, and we again pushed on as we best could. When about a mile from the halting place, the wind rose of a sudden, and we were nearly smothered with sand, which filled eyes, nose and ears, and penetrated to the body through the clothes. It gave me an idea of what a simoom must be. Several marches of a like kind followed, unrelieved by any incident save the mirages by which we were deceived—one in particular so thoroughly resembled a sea that I could not be persuaded but that we were approaching the coast. At length we came in sight of the ruins of ancient Ispahan. Soon after, on reaching the top of a hill, we could see the city which now bears its name lying at our feet. Like Shiraz, the country about it for several miles was dotted with large gardens. But it had a beauty which Shiraz did not possess, for behind it there rose a range of lofty mountains whose rugged sides and snow-capped summits could be descried from the point at which we stood. I stopped for some time to view the scene and give the horses a rest, the hill which we had just climbed having been a stiff one, and then pushed on for the city. It was my intention to put up with the superintendent of the telegraph station. I gave Hagee his name; but as it sounded somewhat like "priest," he misapprehended my meaning, and took me to the mission-house. My surprise was great when I found myself in the presence of a clerical-looking gentleman, who, seeing that there was some mistake, introduced himself as the missionary, and at once offered me the hospitality of his home. I readily accepted it, though I doubt whether I should have done so had I at the time known that he had established a fever hospital within a few yards of his residence. He himself had had the fever—famine fever. He was only just recovered, and had still to wear a skull-cap, his head having had to be shaved during his illness. I inspected the hospital, and the sight of its fever-stricken inmates brought painfully home to my mind what my own fate might be if attacked with sickness in such a place. I was, therefore, not unnaturally anxious to get away from Ispahan with all possible speed. Not so Hagee. We were again in a large city. Hagee had a relish for its pleasures, which increased the longer he stayed in it, and had no desire to hasten our departure. He of course promised to look out for cattle. The worth of such promises I could now estimate, and accordingly made up my mind for a halt of a few days, which I spent in a very agreeable manner. My host was a kind and intelligent man. His wife was equally kind, and both did all they could to make my stay comfortable. The contrast in their natures made me often smile. My host, as might be expected in one in his position, was grave and serious, though not severe. His wife was quiet and simple, her whole aim in her conversations being to impress me with the importance of making jam after a method peculiarly her own. She had only one vanity—pride in the goodness of her native servant, in whom, as she implicitly believed, she had inculcated respect for truth and honesty. I did not share her belief.

It was a long time since my toilette had given me either care or trouble. My costume was simple, and I was indifferent to criticism. One thing, however, did puzzle me. Towards the end of the journey to Ispahan I was more than once addressed as " Hagee " by the natives. Now "Hagee" is a title or distinction earned by devout Mussulmans who make the pilgrimage to Mecca. If a Mussulman's circumstances will not allow of his going himself, he can send a person in his stead; but the deputy can only act for one. My servant had filled this office, and had thus acquired the title of Hagee, with the right of wearing a turban of certain dimensions and particular colour. He told me that formerly not more than three out of six returned to their native countries from these pilgrimages, such were the perils to which they were exposed, and so great the mortality from sickness which invariably breaks out amongst them. It is now known that these gatherings at Mecca are a fruitful source of cholera, and that the returning Turkish pilgrims bring it with them to Europe. But I was never at Mecca, and could not, therefore, conceive why I should be addressed as Hagee. The mystery was explained when I was shown up to my room at the mission-house, and saw my reflection in the looking-glass. I was startled at the sight. My face was like a piece of red blotting-paper dipped in water, and my neck was simply black—black almost as Hagee's. He consoled me by the statement that the heat would go out of the face in about twelve days; and this proved to be the case. While at Ispahan I had to substitute for my simple travelling suit of shirt, trousers, and "gievas," a semi-European costume. The coat and leather boots were instruments of torture, and I longed for the time when I could dispense with them. Meanwhile I rode about Ispahan, and found it, like all other Eastern cities, while fair and beautiful-looking at a distance, the reverse of fair and beautiful when subjected to close inspection. Palaces, mosques, domes, and minarets there were in abundance; but all were in a state of decay, and everywhere dirt and misery, disease in the famine-stricken here manifesting itself in terrible boils and sores. Of one charming feature, however, the city could boast—its beautiful gardens, and the quaint bridges which span the river Zeinderoot, on which it is built, also lend to it picturesqueness. The river takes its rise in the mountains to which I have referred, and attains considerable volume from the melting of the snow in the spring. On the bridges men regularly take their stand and furnish pipes to the travellers. I declined the proffered whiff, but Hagee was not so squeamish.

While at Ispahan I dined with the superintendent of the telegraph station. Among the guests was the doctor who had fallen into the hands of the desert marauders. He told me that they had stripped him and compelled him to walk for miles on his bare feet, and that his servants all bolted at the approach of the robbers. Though still suffering from the hardships he had had to endure (he could barely limp), he was full of vivacity, and described with comical effect the stampede amongst his escort, who up to the moment of danger were (self-styled) the bravest men he had ever met. His humour was infectious, but there was also the grave side to his story, which was not without interest for me. An incident occurred after dinner, which also reminded me that I was in the East. My friends, on looking over the cook's accounts, discovered that he had cheated them. Thereupon the other servants, or "ferrashes," were called in; the dishonest cook was seized and taken down into the compound; his feet were tied to a pole; sticks were brought, and the bastinado was administered. It is not, I believe, owing to the hardness of the feet of the natives, as severe a chastisement as Europeans deem it to be. Still, by the beard of the Prophet! I was glad to get out of Ispahan, and marked the date of my departure in red letters as the 28th of April.

Chapter XIII.

ISPAHAN TO RESHT.

OUR march to Gez was not near so tedious or wearisome as those which had preceded it. Numerous gardens were passed, patches of verdure were also here and there to be seen; and if shade were not to be had, there was, at all events, something on which the eye could rest with pleasure. Gez is celebrated for its manna. I got some and relished it very much. It is plucked from bushes, and almonds and sugar are mixed with it, making on the whole a rather sweet compound. When very thirsty I used to suck a little, and found it very refreshing, but care has to be taken that it does not melt in the package. Kashan was likewise reached, but after weary marches, and then followed the journey of several hundred miles to

Teheran, over vast sandy deserts and salt plains. It was almost a repetition of that which we made between Shiraz and Ispahan. But the marches were longer and more fatiguing, the sun grew hotter and hotter, the salt plains intensified our thirst, and dead bodies in every stage of decomposition became more and more frequent. Upon these vultures gorged, unheeding the traveller, or flying away on lazy wing to a little distance until he passed. The unhappy beings who thus perished on the desert plains were doubtless driven from their own mountain homes or villages by want, and were on their way to some one of the chief towns of the country, in the hope of finding there the food for which they starved. They lay where they fell exhausted, and found in death relief from their sufferings. At Shiraz, Kazeroon, Ispahan and Teheran I saw food, purchased out of the funds forwarded by the " Persian Relief Fund Committee," which was formed in London, distributed in large quantities among the people. At Ispahan the missionary with whom I stopped was indefatigable in his exertions to relieve them; but the distress was too great and widespread, the population too scattered, the means of local organization too slender, to give hope that those charitable efforts met with the success which they deserved. The proximate cause of the famine was the little snow which fell in 1870 and the want of rain in 1871. Whether the Government of the Shah realised its full extent, or what means were taken by them to meet it, I know not. I only know that during the time of which I speak the sufferings of those over whom he rules were such as can only be witnessed in the East or borne by an Asiatic people.

The difficulty of getting horses at the stations at which we halted continued to increase. Those, too, which we did succeed in procuring were of the poorest kind, and it was accordingly no infrequent occurrence for one of them to drop dead on the march. We had then to shift or distribute his pack and push on, sometimes on foot, as we best could. When driven to this the salt plains were the most distressing ground to be traversed, the heat of the sun on them far exceeding that which is experienced on the sandy desert. At length, after a journey of over 700 miles, we reached Teheran, and put up with the superintendent of the Telegraph Station. Teheran being the capital of Persia, there is of course a British Mission at it. Russia and France, and I think also Germany, have likewise Missions at it, and some forty or fifty Europeans reside at the place. About five miles to the south of it the ruins of the city of Rae, which holds a distinguished place in Persian history, are still to be seen. On the north the mountain of Demavend, which is said to be 15,000 feet high, raises its snow-capped top above the plain. A lofty range of mountains which are known as the Elburz, and, like the Hartz in Germany, are supposed by the Persians to be the abode of demons, lie on the east, and a plain of vast extent stetches away to the west. The town itself is three or four miles in circumference, and is surrounded by a high wall flanked with many towers. The palace, which was built by Kurrim Khan, and enlarged by the present Shah, is an imposing structure. It is of great size, and its varied orders of architecture are outnumbered only by its colours, which are those of the rainbow. The bazaar surpassed all which I had previously seen, and the streets are also broader, and in every respect much better than those of Shiraz or Ispahan. Being just on the border-line of civilization, Persia must, of course, have the expensive European luxury of a standing army. The troops stationed at Teheran were paraded and drilled every morning during my stay in the city, and nothing could exceed the horrible din which they made with their drums and trumpets, which, like their uniforms and arms, seemed to have been principally brought from Russia. The drummers banged their drums, and the trumpeters blew their trumpets, and the contest between them seemed to be which could make the most noise. The system under which the bastinado flourished would, I thought, be preferable to this parody of Europe. A more musical ear might have detected something to admire in these Persian military bands, but their effect on me was to hasten my departure from the capital.

It might be supposed that here, at least, horses could easily be had. By no means. It was only after several days' search that any could be found, and the agreement with the owner as to the rate of hire and the time within which the journey was to be performed became then as difficult and prolonged as the settlement of an international dispute. As is the case in such questions, also, a loophole was left in the agreement into which I now entered, and, to follow out the simile, it became first the subject of arbitration and then the cause of war. The case was this: the contractor or owner of the horses agreed to lend me three—one for myself, one for Hagee, and one for himself; that he should take me to Resht within eleven days, and that if he failed in this particular he should forfeit half the contract-money. Meantime, while our preparations for the journey were being made, a European gentleman, a friend of my host, called one evening at the station, and after stating that he had heard I was bound for Resht, proposed that I should join a party consisting of one or two ladies, a few children, and an old gentleman, who were also about to start for Europe. Reduced to plain terms, the proposition was that I should be their escort. I confess I was not gratified with it. A feeling of gallantry and goodnature prompted me to say "yes," while prudence dictated "no," because, though the route now before me was not so difficult or dangerous as that which I had already traversed, yet there was more risk in travelling with a caravan than with my own small party, and I shrank from undertaking the responsibility. In addition, time was of consequence to me. I could not, however, well refuse, and, after the matter had been once or twice discussed, consented to form one of the Mission Caravan, as it was called. It started on the 12th of May. We were behind time, Hagee being drunk and the contractor dilatory. We did not, in consequence, get away until noon. Dull, and nearly silent for the whole of the march, we rode on throughout the day and far into the night, when I was startled by a shout from Hagee, who conveyed to me the gratifying intelligence that we had wandered from the track. I had been feverish all the day; the night air had refreshed me, but I was still weak and unwell, and longed for rest. The blunder of the contractor was not calculated to increase my good spirits, and I gave expression to my irritation in language more emphatic than choice. The track was again found after some search, but it was so very late when we reached the chappar khaneh, that we lay down to rest after we had had a hasty meal and the horses had also been fed.

The march was resumed next morning about 11 o'clock, and we pushed on to overtake the Mission Caravan, which had got a slight start of us. We hoped to come up with them at their middle halt, which would be about 3 o'clock, as, like ourselves, they had been also late in their departure. About seven miles from the khaneh Hagee's horse showed signs of giving in. My own horse had little to boast over it, while the one which the contractor had reserved for himself—and this I had early noticed with no little chagrin —was much superior to either. The time had now come for a change. I therefore let him know that I would not stand a twelve hours' march when the distance could be done in much less time, and ended by demanding his horse for Hagee. But this he declined to do. Greatly enraged, I called upon Hagee to help me to throw him off; but Hagee, who, notwithstanding his fierce look and actual strength, had something of the coward at heart, deemed prudence the better part of valour, and declared for neutrality. It may be that he was influenced by the fact that the contractor was accompanied by a fellow Persian to aid him in bringing back the horses from Resht, and that the fight might therefore be too even to be safe. This man, by the way, was a wonderful walker. Day after day would he hold on at our pace on the march, and be able to jump anything within reason at the end of it. But to resume. Determined to enforce the demand once I had made it, I rushed at and nearly unhorsed the contractor, but with the agility of the Persian horseman he was again in the saddle in a moment, and darting his heels into his horse's flanks, put some twenty yards between us. The sight of my revolver, which I now drew, was the signal for a wild dash to a village which lay about a mile off across the plain. The temptation to take a flying shot at him was great, but my anger did not extend to the horse, and the thought that I might strike it rather than its owner restrained me. About an hour afterwards we saw him behind another man on the top of a trotting camel (a rare thing in Persia), and he looked so ridiculous with his robes flying about him that it was impossible not to be moved to laughter. On passing us, but at a respectful distance, he shouted out to Hagee that he was going to the Feringhee Sahib of the caravan, to tell him what I had done and to ask him to settle the dispute between us. The caravan was now in sight, and when we came up with it the main body were enjoying the middle halt under the shade of some trees in a " garden." The so-called gardens are in reality but clumps of trees. They give, however, good shade, and no one can tell what a luxury it is who has not seethed under a Persian sun. You need but look at their spreading branches and the patch of verdure beneath them, and then cast your eye on the burning sands, stretching on every side about them, to realize why poetic imagery has been called in aid of their description, and why they are termed "oases in the desert."

The party of which I was to form one for the remainder of my journey to Enzelli was now before me. The ladies, three in number, were seated on a carpet, which was spread beneath a large tree. Two little girls, about six and seven years of age respectively, were playing about some little distance off; and in the back ground, the servant who had charge of them, and who was rather a pretty young girl of twenty, was talking to another of her sex and class, much her senior in years, and of stiff and prudish appearance. The gentleman of the party, who was between fifty and sixty years of age, was leisurely sauntering about, and as apparently unmoved by the scene as if he were lounging in the Broadway, New York. I say the Broadway, because the party, with one exception, had really come from the other side of the Atlantic to Teheran to attend at the deathbed-side of a distant relative or connection, but who died unmindful of his obligations to them, and left all his property to an Armenian with whom he had lived in Persia. With the elasticity of their people, they did not dwell upon their disappointment; and if I had not been told their story, I should never have dreamt that they had journeyed some thousands of miles by land and sea to Persia—from the chief city of the greatest empire of the New World to the capital of the representative nation of the most powerful monarchy of the old—to receive a justly-expected legacy, and that they returned without the gift. I was, of course, immediately recognized and welcomed as one of themselves, and, with the freedom of travellers, we soon became intimate. The old gentleman, whom I shall call Mr. A., was of an imperative temper, but amusing. Cyrus himself could not have given his orders with more authority. "This thou shalt do," and "this thou shalt not do;" so he commanded the caravan, and was obeyed. When on the march, he sat taciturn and erect in his saddle, and defied the elements—air, earth, fire and water—with an enormous umbrella. His wife, one of the two ladies I have mentioned, was also rather advanced in years, but still retained traces of her early beauty, and humoured her irritable and imperial spouse with true womanly tact. The second lady was their widowed daughter, and the third was the wife of a European gentleman resident at Teheran, and now on her way to Europe. The little girls were the grandchildren of the aged couple, and upon them the grandfather lavished all the wealth of his affection, and it was great; for although testy, he was still of a kindly nature. The little ones were pretty and cheerful, and enlivened the way by the pranks and tricks which they played upon the old man, whom they styled the "cross old Badger," and who looked the character, but did not act up to it. The maid was short and plump— Sarah, the prude, tall and gaunt. Her charms were heightened by just a suspicion of a moustache: and, at first sight, she made such an impression on Hagee, that he was her humble and devoted slave to the end of our journey. The caravan was also accompanied by a little Persian gentleman, whose acquaintance my friends had made at Teheran, and who appeared very loth that they should part. He was about 4 feet 3 inches in height, of slight build, and dusky complexion, and was the son of a Persian grandee, who was dead. He dressed like a Persian "swell," chastised his "gholam" as a man of his high rank but few inches should do (the "gholam" seemed rather to like him the more for it), was always in good spirits, and was the most agreeable of travelling companions. He spoke a little English, and we got on very well together, pipes and conversation shortening the miles and cheering the way. My friend the contractor appeared on the scene shortly after I had joined the caravan. He was ordered to come before the Feringhee Sahib (Mr. A.), and stated his case with much art and colouring. The judgment, however, went against him, and then away again he bolted on the trotting camel, mindful, no doubt, that his horse was beyond the reach of capture, and that he had the contract-money in his pocket. There still remained with us the two horses on which Hagee and myself rode. The "deputy," in consequence, hung on to the caravan, and never seemed distressed at its pace or length of march.

Refreshed by the halt, the journey was resumed with good spirits. The two gentlemen of the caravan and one of the ladies were mounted on good horses. The rest of the party were in a "tachteravan," a description of conveyance or covered litter used by Persian women while travelling. It is a box about seven feet long by four feet broad, and about four feet high. It has a door on each side, sliding in a longitudinal direction, so that if in crossing a mountain pass one side of the conveyance should get jammed against a rock, there is still a way out on the other side. Light is admitted by windows in the top, and the litter itself is carried on two long poles, which project at either end and are fastened to two mules, one in front, the other behind. Two men are required to look after the vehicle—one to guide the leading mule, the other to help the mule behind and steady the box. The two servants were in " kejavas," which are somewhat like English panniers. They are covered all over, except in front, with blue cloth, and are mounted by means of a ladder. The mule which carried the "kejavas" had also its driver. The cook, who was the "comic man" among the Persians attached to the caravan, carried behind the pack on his mule a lighted fire like that which I saw with the party I met on leaving Shiraz. From it he supplied them with hot embers for their "kalians," and always before the halt galloped ahead of the caravan in order to get the "samavar," or Russian urn, ready for the tea, a cup of which always proved most refreshing. When the halt was called the "tachteravan" was lowered to the ground, a ladder was rested against the panniers, and Hagee, availing himself of the opportunity to display his gallantry, assisted Sarah to alight, an attention with which she was much flattered. The evening meal was a far more sumptuous repast than any I had been accustomed to in my solitary marches. I did not object to it—in fact I relished it, but all my notions of propriety as a traveller were outraged by the sight at the khaneh of an iron bedstead and mattress, with pillows and blankets. It was some satisfaction, however, to note that the walls of the room were more than ordinarily black and dirty, and to be requested by the ladies to smoke a cigar in it as a corrective to the vile smells which pervaded the place. We had scarcely reached our quarters for the night, when one of the most violent storms of thunder and lightning which I had ever witnessed burst upon the plain. In the women it excited a feeling of intense terror. They cried and moaned, and hid their faces in the bedclothes, responding to each deafening peal with a shriek of agony. The men of the party stood at the door of the khaneh watching the play of the lightning, which was intensely vivid. It was impossible to resist a feeling of awe in beholding such a war of the elements, and the deep silence which prevailed among our party showed that all shared in it. Happily, the storm was soon over, but the impression which it made upon all was not soon forgotten. A quiet smoke and a chat with Mr. A. brought the day's labour to a close. Finding sleep impossible in the khaneh, owing to its insufferable odours and closeness, I went out on the plain and took up my quarters in the "tachteravan," having first dispossessed two Persians who occupied it, and who were consoled with the gift of a "khran" for being disturbed. The dangers of the situation, for I was outside the walls, and the protection of the khaneh, were soon forgotten. The croaking of countless frogs in some stagnant water close by was also unheeded, and the sleep for which I longed came gratefully to my eyes. I woke refreshed early in the morning, and was the first abroad. Soon after, the khaneh was all astir. Coffee was got ready, the animals were fed and packed, and all the preparations made for the march. It was a tedious business. When alone, thirty minutes from the time I was aroused by my servant would see us on the march. Now it took fully two hours to get our caravan in motion.

The start was at last made. The Mission Caravan took the upper track, in order to avoid the low ground which had been rendered swampy by the overnight's rain. As we drew away from Teheran the more painful sights of the famine began to diminish. The evidences of want and suffering were still numerous; but dead bodies did not mark the way as between Ispahan and the capital. We could note also that the corpses were not, as at other places, allowed to lie and rot on the plains a prey to the ravenous dog and foul vulture. The rites of sepulture were now given to them. A grave was dug in the sands, and, where water could be had, the body was washed before being lowered into its last resting-place. This washing of the body before interment possessed a touching interest. No sign of mourning was shewn by those who assisted at the rite, but it was the only mark of respect which they could pay to their departed relative or friend; and in these districts, apparently, where it was possible to observe it, it was never forgotten. The marches, though still laborious, were now at least pleasant; but an incident which occurred on this day's journey warned us that the danger from predatory bands was not passed. The caravan straggled after the middle halt. The horsemen were far in advance, the animals with the packs almost out of sight in the rear. No better opportunity could be offered for a raid. It was seen and availed of by a few marauders, who darted from their lair and fell on the Persians in charge of the straggling mules. These, happily, offered every resistance, though on such occasions their habit is to bolt, and their motto, " every man for himself." The alarm was also rapidly passed along the line. Others of the caravan hastened to the assistance of their fellows, and the robbers made off without accomplishing their purpose. Shots were interchanged between the combatants, but on our side, happily, without any fatal or serious result. The Persians of the caravan, however, who were engaged in the *mêlée*, declared that it could not have been the case with their assailants, inasmuch as it could be clearly seen that one of the bandits could with difficulty keep his seat on his horse as he galloped across the plain.

As we advanced, small rivers and streams had frequently to be crossed. The first which we forded was about twenty or thirty yards broad, and was much swollen by the rains. The horsemen first tried its depth and strength in order to judge whether the rest of the caravan could safely pass it. The appearance of the banks showed that the stream was much above its level, and its rapid flow gave warning that it was not to be forded without risk. Counsel was taken upon the subject. The horsemen had little to fear; the danger was for the women and children. A suggestion of mine, to pass a rope diagonally across the stream, and to attach the "tachteravan" to it by means of a second rope with a running knot, which would serve as a guide, was unheeded as an unnecessary precaution, and the mules were led into the water, which they were ignorantly made to breast. The leading mule was soon above its belly in the stream, and was struggling hard to keep its footing. The rushing water also caught the bottom of the "tachteravan," and all expected to see it either turned over or swept into a "cannon," or deep pool, which lay a little farther down the stream. The occupants of the vehicle were pale with terror, but too frightened to cry. Bravely did the mules struggle, making their way foot by foot, and holding their ground with the tenacity displayed by them on the mountain paths. In such emergencies it is always advisable to leave them to themselves. Their own instinct is their best guide, and interference will impede rather than assist their efforts. A few minutes of breathless suspense, mingled with admiration for the patient and courageous animals, and the danger was passed, to the joy and relief of all. Then came the turn of the "kejavas." The child's maid laughed; Sarah, the second servant, shrieked; and Hagee, who cherished, I think, the hope of placing her at the head of the list of his wives, swore at the muleteers in a compound of English and Persian, in a way which caused them to tremble, and provoked the Europeans of the party to shouts of laughter. The passage of the cook, in whose welfare, by the way, we all took the deepest interest, seeing how much he ministered to our comforts, was also of a kind to excite mirth. He appeared to have a presentiment of his fate. His face grew pale almost to ghastliness, and he approached the water with caution and timidity. The fire carried at the pack also gave him concern, and he was distracted between watching it and the movements of his mule. Scarcely had he got into the stream when the mule stumbled, and its luckless rider disappeared in the water. But up he came again, yelling for help, and minus his skull cap, looking the picture of comical terror. He stuck to the mule, and called upon the Prophet, and then upon Hagee, for assistance. His hopes, however, clearly rested upon Hagee. But Hagee was consoling Sarah, and heeded not his cries. His poor and heavily-laden beast was his best friend. Hanging on to it, he got over in safety, but with the loss of some of his cooking utensils, a circumstance which brought back gravity to all our countenances. However, our danger and our loss were soon forgotten, and the march was resumed with fresh spirits. In the course of it and a few succeeding marches several very peculiar mounds were passed. They, were of conical shape, from fifty to sixty feet high, and at the base about 300 feet in diameter. They stood about four miles apart, and extended over a track of perhaps forty miles. We questioned the natives with the caravan as to their character, but could obtain no information respecting them. Our own knowledge of the history and antiquities of the country was too slight to enable us even to speculate upon their object or purpose.

The Mission Caravan had before leaving Teheran obtained from the Shah permission to occupy where they halted any one's house they pleased. We were still in the East, you see, though now close up to the border line on the other side of which Romance lay buried, and vulgar Reality, relieved to be sure by a respect for *meum* and *tuum*, flourished. When, then, we came to a village where the caravansary was of a very ruinous kind, we looked about for the best house in the place, proclaiming our intention and the Shah's behests. The house was shut up. But what of that? Let the "head-man" of the village be summoned and let the place be opened. It was opened. I did not rest in it myself, but my friends did. We thus journeyed on from day to day, but not wearily, for we were now traversing the rich provinces of Persia, and found plenty to attract our attention as well as excite our admiration. One march, however, was rendered memorable by a hailstorm which I shall not readily forget. Its approach was startling. The wind was in our teeth, and we noticed that far away in the quarter from which it blew the clouds were thick and black. On a sudden a sound like a roar was heard in the air. It came nearer and nearer, growing louder as it did, and inspired all the caravan with a feeling of terror, for nothing could be seen to which the noise could be attributed. The horses and mules stood still and trembled. It was as if some dreadful convulsion were about to take place. The roar still became greater, so much so that I could not make Hagee hear me though only a few yards off, and then what looked like a wall of rain came dashing towards us. At sight of it the animals became uncontrollable. They reared and bounded with terror, and though jaded, several of them broke away and dashed across the plain. We were now in the very midst of the storm. The hail descended in showers and beat on us with terrific force. I experienced its full fury, my dress consisting only of the few and light garments which I have already mentioned. I made my way with difficulty to Hagee and got a rug which I threw over my shoulders. I could not, however, cover my head or face owing to the plunging of my horse, and I was so bruised and hurt from the hailstones, which were like lumps of ice, that tears came into my eyes. Some of the muleteers threw themselves on the ground and began to pray; others were wildly rushing after the animals which had stampeded. The storm lasted about fifteen minutes—the most miserable quarter of an hour I had ever spent in my life. When it passed over I looked about for the "tachteravan," and descried it far ahead. On coming up to it I learned from its occupants that they too had suffered from the storm, but happily not to the same extent as the main body of the caravan, over which it broke and spent its fury. The windows of the "tachteravan" were, however, broken, and its roof was marked like a rifle target. The ladies were pale and silent—the children in tears. The storm was the topic of conversation for several days afterwards, during which we were haunted with the apprehension that it foreboded some such convulsion of nature as that which had proved so disastrous to Shiraz in 1852. Its effects gradually wore away, and with them also the fears to which it gave rise.

After fording several small streams we again got to the mountains. The ascents were very steep, and the occupants of the "tachteravan" had an exciting time of it. The paths were often only a few feet wide, and wound round many sharp projections of rock. At these times the "tachteravan" literally hung over the abyss beneath, and it required more nerve than the ladies possessed to sit unmoved in it. They therefore got out of the conveyance, preferring to undergo all the fatigues of the ascent on foot rather than hang suspended like Mahomet's coffin between earth and heaven. They were not, however, without compensation. The scenery was of the wildest character. Rock was piled upon rock in fantastic confusion; precipices lay on every side straight and steep as if the mountain had been cleft at one blow; peaks which would tempt a member of the Alpine Club towered aloft, and far above them the snow glistened and marked the summit of the range. Walking, they could behold and enjoy these sights, and it was not until they were exhausted by the toil of climbing that the " tachteravan" was used, and then with regret.

A long time was occupied in crossing this chain of mountains, but the views were so beautiful that all sense of fatigue was lost in beholding them. The plain on which we descended was dotted with mounds and hills of a deep red colour. The rocks, too, gave every indication of ironstone, and so far as my experience enabled me to judge, the plain abounded in minerals. If my surmise should prove correct, and this part of Persia should be opened up by English enterprise, the speculator will find his gain in the plain of which I speak. A march or so from it we crossed a river and followed its banks, which were thickly grown with reeds and grass, for several days. Clumps of trees were also frequently met with, but the heat became again excessive, and the halts were welcomed by all. On re-crossing the river, which we did not by fording, but by a very primitive and decayed bridge, we reached the rich and low-lying country which surrounds Resht, and during these marches most of our party took quinine freely to guard against the malaria which breeds fever and ague. Having little faith in physic I barely tasted it, and relied upon care and a good constitution for my safety. At one point, however, our camping-ground was chosen in such defiance of all sanitary principles that we had nearly suffered from our imprudence or ignorance. It was about thirty or forty feet below the level of the track on which we had been travelling, and between it and the river there lay a rank and dense jungle. The undergrowth beneath the trees whose shade we sought was also excessive, and while the meridian sun shone upon it the whole place steamed. All in consequence complained of lassitude. We were parched with thirst, but the water was too bad to drink, and the tea which the cook soon prepared, though refreshing, brought with it profuse perspiration. Sarah, the servant, who was helped out of the "kejavas" with all tenderness by Hagee, was seized with illness and began to cry. Hagee himself also looked as if all were not right with him. His face had assumed a greyish colour. Soon after he began to retch violently, and lay down, apparently in great distress. I was naturally concerned for him, for he had been to me as much a companion in my travels as a servant. Fearing that his attack might be one of cholera, I got my medicine-chest, small, but sufficient for my purposes, and offered to prescribe for him, but he thought brandy would be better than physic. I in vain represented to him the danger of taking so fiery a spirit and having afterwards to march under a blazing sun, and so let him have the brandy, which, as I expected, made him still more ill. The troubles of the halt were not yet over. The horse, a rather spirited animal, of our Persian friend, took fright and broke loose and dashed through the caravan, to the imminent risk of all. The crashing of some branches within a few yards of me gave me warning of his approach, and I had barely time to jump to my feet when he was down upon me. He fortunately stumbled and rolled over at the moment, and was secured before he could again get away. The concern of the owner extended rather to his bridle and saddle than to the animal itself. "My bridle—my saddle—he will run away with them!" formed the burden of his cry as he rushed to the spot where the panting horse lay, and great was his joy on finding that neither of his treasures was injured. When the halt was over Hagee could with difficulty mount his horse, but anxiety to leave the place banished from our minds every other care, and a few hours' more marching brought us in safety to an Illiat camp, the first which we had yet seen.

It consisted of about a dozen tents made of black cloth, with matting round the sides. The people seemed very hospitable, and freely gave goat's milk to the men of the caravan. Another agreeable feature about them was the kindness they showed to their dogs. In the south the dog is considered and treated as an abomination—worse even than the leper. Among the hill tribes, as with all who follow a pastoral life, he becomes once more man's companion and most trusty servant, needing no master's eye while watching his flocks. He is therefore respected and treated well. Those which I saw resembled our own sheep dogs, and are equally useful and brave, but much fiercer. In some parts of the country, and especially in those districts given to the breeding of horses, the pig is also viewed with some degree of favour. The Persians believe that it keeps disease away from all other cattle, and therefore keep swine in their stables. While travelling among the Illiat tribes we were always able to procure some description of milk—that of the goat, the ewe, the cow, or the mare. The goat's milk is a little thicker and richer than that of the cow. It has a peculiar taste, and in the case of some breeds is so strong as to be disagreeable. The butter, as also the cheese, made from it is whiter than that made from the milk of the cow. Ewe's milk is also too rich to be palatable, and the mare's and ass's milk which I drank I thought very distasteful. Camel's milk I also tried, but found it very sickly and nauseous. An opinion prevails that the camel is not capable of bearing much cold. My experience could not confirm it, for I have seen them looking well on the high lands of Persia, where the thermometer during the night at certain periods of the year is little above the freezing point.

After passing these wanderers we came to the brow of a hill, from which we could descry our destination for the night. The villagers had seen us in the distance, and assembled to witness our entry. It proved to be one of the testing stations of the Telegraph Company, and was, of course, in charge of an Armenian, who was assisted in the performance of his duty by an old and crippled negro. The village was encircled by large woods, which further on assumed the dimensions of a forest, and a pleasant brook also ran through it. After a refreshing dip in its waters, I went in search of Hagee, and found him still very ill—so ill that he was quite willing to try the contents of the medicine-chest. I accordingly dosed him well, and had the satisfaction of finding him next morning in his wonted health and spirits. We had for some time remarked with pleasure that the signs of the famine were rapidly decreasing, but the appearance of the villagers told us that we were still within its limits. The khaneh at which we halted was besieged by them begging for food, and a young girl, who was still good-looking, though very worn and thin, and who sat in silence and sadness some distance from the brook, ravenously ate the bread which I sent to her by Hagee. At the next night's halt my skill as a physician was again called into requisition. A man was bitten by a snake, and Hagee besought me to see and cure him. The man himself also sent supplicating my aid. I knew of no medicine in my chest which could be used on such an occasion, but thought of a remedy that was practised in a case of snake-poisoning which I witnessed in the woods of New Brunswick. The remedy there adopted was whisky, which the patient was compelled to drink in large quantities. To use a common but expressive phrase, he was in fact "drowned" in it. On going to the man I found that a ligature made of a leather thong had been tied above the elbow, and that the lower part of the arm where the snake had bitten him was swollen to an enormous size. He drank the brandy which

I gave him, but refused a second cupful (my iron cup was the measure), as the liquor had scorched his throat. On representing to him, however, that it was the only chance of saving his life, he swallowed the second dose. I heard next morning that he was living and lying out on the plain, and still under the influence of his potations. News of a different character, but not altogether unexpected, also awaited me, namely, that during the night one of my horses had died. Fortunately, however, I was able to procure another at the khaneh, and had not, therefore, to delay our departure.

The next march but one brought us to the forest, and nothing could be more agreeable than the journey through it. Its shade was delightful, and with the memory of sterile plains and deserts to heighten the contrast, its green and luxuriant foliage had an indescribable charm for the eye. The houses, which were now pretty numerous, were no longer made of mud but of wood, which gave them a cheerful appearance, and the track gradually developed into a road, at the sides of which lay stagnant pools of water which were literally alive with tortoise. Some were as small as the centre of a saucer, others as large as a dinner plate. They basked in hundreds at the edges of the pools, and it was amusing to observe the "skedaddle"—it is the only word that can describe the rush—which took place on the noise of our approach. I surprised and captured one by turning it on its back, but the endeavour to catch them by hand is dangerous pastime, for the water also abounds with snakes. So numerous, indeed, are the reptiles in this quarter, that we were told a caravansary which we had passed had been rendered uninhabitable by their presence. On reaching it, however, I observed a few people lying asleep in front of it, but their lot was possibly so wretched as to make them indifferent to the consequences of sharing their home with vipers. On emerging from the forest after a few days' march, we came upon large clearings in which rice was being cultivated in swampy fields, and travelled along a tolerable road lined with trees in very great variety. They included the cypress and the cedar, several kinds of pine, limes, acacias, chestnuts, and several specimens of the manna ash. Resht at last came into sight, and we were here met by the resident consul, who rode out to meet us and invite us to share the hospitality of his home. We were soon housed at the Consulate, a plain and rather cheerless building, and early next morning were ready to start for Pyr-i-Bazaar, where we were to embark in the boats which were to take us down the lagune to Enzelli.

Chapter XIV.

RESHT TO ENZELLI.

IN an earlier part of my narrative, I mentioned my dispute with the "contractor," its reference to arbitration, and the judgment of the arbitrator in my favour—a judgment which bore no fruit, inasmuch as the "contractor" bolted the moment it was delivered. I also stated that, notwithstanding the arbitration, the quarrel was unsettled, and that it ultimately led to war. The time had now arrived when hostilities were to commence. The contractor himself vanished, as I have said; his deputy remained with us, accompanying us across the plains and over the mountain passes with an endurance which seemed incapable of breaking down. He now came prominently on the scene, determined to play out the part allotted to him. When we were all ready to start for the boats, he demanded the extra sum which I had promised to pay for the hire of the horses, always provided that the contract was fulfilled to my satisfaction. But the contract was not so fulfilled. Not only did the contractor refuse the use of the only serviceable horse of the three which he had hired to me and ride off with it at the last, but those which he left were so poor, and in such wretched condition, that it was a labour to Hagee and myself to keep our place in the caravan. The demand in consequence appeared to me in the light of extortion, and I flatly refused to comply with it. It was repeated with insolence, and was again met with a refusal. In this mood we left the town, the Persian following at my horse's heels. I had to wait for Hagee, who had been overnight indulging in his propensity for strong drink, and was not even now sober. I was in consequence far in the rear of the caravan. The Persian saw all this, and resolved to make the most of the opportunity. Accordingly, I had scarcely got clear of the narrow streets of the town than he seized my horse by the bridle. I made signs to him to loose his hold, and as he would not, gave him a smart cut with my whip, which also had no effect. A blow on the wrist followed, and the vigour with which I sought to administer a third, but which he avoided by ducking, nearly unhorsed me. He still retained his hold of the bridle, and hissed at me, with every expression of insolence and rage, the contemptuous epithet of his country, " Padre S-Ag" (son of a dog). In a moment I was out of the saddle, and punished the fellow with a "facer," which caused him to measure his length on the ground. I re-mounted, but could not get the horse to stir, and in a few seconds was again on the ground, this time at full length, the Persian having seized me by the leg and thrown me out of the saddle. I was stunned, but not hurt. On rising, I saw him fumbling behind his back for his knife, but before he could draw it I closed with him. We were now fairly in the lists. My superior in size and strength, I relied upon some skill which I had acquired at home as a wrestler, but could not use it to the best advantage, as I had to employ all my efforts either to secure the knife for myself, or to prevent him from drawing it. In the struggle we stumbled and fell. He was uppermost, but I had a firm grasp of the knife. Holding me with all his might, he got his knees on my breast, and sought to strangle me. At this moment two of the town guards came galloping towards us, riding so recklessly that it seemed to me they would trample upon us both, and put an end to the combat in a way which neither Englishman nor Persian dreamt of when it was commenced. This, however, they did not. They passed on either side of us, and I became all but unconscious. What actually occurred I cannot say. I only know that my assailant was lifted off me, and that I myself managed somehow to get on to my feet. Hagee then came up, and was valiant when the fray was over. On arriving at Pyr-i-Bazaar, where the boats awaited us, the Persian again appeared and repeated his demand. I took no notice of him; but while helping Hagee to unload the horses and stow our luggage in the boat, quietly prepared for a renewal of the combat. The other members of the caravan were already in their boats, and had pushed off from the landing-place, leaving me to settle my controversy with the Persian as I best could, although I had fully explained to them the point at issue between us, and that it had already been determined in my favour by Mr. A. It may be that, if things had come to the worst, Mr. A. would have been of little assistance to me in the crowd of people who were gathered together at the place of embarkation; but the complete indifference which he and the other members of the party showed as to my fate stung me to the quick, and put me thoroughly on my mettle. The minutes flew fast; and when all was ready for the start, and I was about to get on board the boat, the Persian stepped forward, encouraged by the shouts of his friends, and seized me by the collar. I was prepared for such a movement on his part. My revolvers were slung ready at my waist. Seizing one, I quietly, but determinedly, put the muzzle to his head. The effect was as I expected. His grip relaxed and his friends were silent. Hagee now became the hostage. The sight of the "barker" also effected his release, and a few seconds after we were out of the reach of all further molestation, and rowing hard after the other boats, which were far in advance, and lost behind a bend of the lagune. What traveller is there who has not had his pleasures marred by such incidents? The demand may be trifling, the overcharge small, but pride, or a feeling very like it, steps in and says, "Do not yield—you are no man if you do." But passion cannot last always; and when it has passed away you recall the occasions on which your generosity has amounted to extravagance, and compare them with those on which your punctiliousness or economy has almost descended to the level of meanness. The retrospect is never agreeable. It brought to me the reverse of a pleasant state of mind. I felt that I had been impetuous, perhaps ungenerous, but then I could not admit that I had been in the wrong. It was a case of the sun and wind trying their strength on the traveller. Had the Persian appealed to my generosity, I should, in all probability, have given him the gratuity; demanded as a right, I resisted it. However, there was now no remedy for the past, and the scene through which we were passing claimed attention.

Pyr-i-Bazaar is a short march from Resht, and consists of some dozen huts and stores built at the head of a lagune. As we rowed down it the place seemed alive with wild duck and water-fowl, the little fear which they evinced at our approach being proof that they were not often disturbed by the gun of the sportsman. After awhile some of the crew landed and towed us along the banks, during which time I sought to recover my good humour by indulgence in the pipe and abuse of Hagee, who was penitent and silent. The muleteers were also in the boat, their contract being to accompany the caravan to Enzelli, for the purpose of helping the "gholams" in the shipping and unshipping of the luggage. They all appeared to enjoy the change from the burning plain to the refreshing sea; but the most joyous amongst them was a Hindoo who could speak a little English, and who had wandered from Bombay to Bushire in a way which he himself could not explain. The shore was almost hidden by reeds and water-plants. Here and there clearings were made which served as harbours for boats, and the huts were also numerous. Bathing seemed to be a pastime amongst the people. We passed many parties of both sexes disporting themselves in the water, and envied them the pleasures of the bath, for the sun was hot, and we were covered with the sands of the desert. Sail was hoisted on clearing the lagune, and with a smart breeze we made rapid way through narrow channels and by many small islands, which seemed to be the resort of millions of sea-birds. In their flight when massed together they appeared like clouds, and shut off the sun's rays from our boat. Magnificent forests, which came down to the water's edge, extended as far as the eye could reach. It was pleasure—such a pleasure as only those who have had to traverse arid and sandy wastes for any time can feel—to behold them. Their beauty seemed to me indescribable; and in this mood we sailed along, taking little heed of what there was of commonplace in the scene. Amongst these was a ship-building yard, evidently a Government establishment, without a ship. But the spectacle was not unusual at home, and I was not surprised at it in the Shah's dominions. Further on lay his yacht at a quay built on piles. She was a paddle steamer of about 200 tons burden, and, like the palace at Tcheran, was sadly in want of a coat of paint. We cleared the lagune shortly afterwards, and then entered the harbour of Enzelli, the chief Persian port on the Caspian Sea.

The Mission Caravan had authority to put up at the Shah's palace, which is built in a large garden planted with orange and lemon-trees and a variety of shrubs, and commands a view of the sea. Thither Hagee and myself went, but were told that there was no room, which was a palpable fib, as the place was spacious enough to accommodate a couple of hundred of people. Time did not admit of argument or remonstrance, so we fell back on the caravansary, which was luxurious to the ones we had occupied in the desert, and was crowded with merchants of many nations. Balconies were carried round the building; in these the guests were lounging, and the place seemed a perfect Babel, so many and so different were the tongues to be heard as we entered it. In the yard or compound the hubbub was even greater. It resembled a fair. Sale and barter were being actively carried on, and the uproar was like the clamour which may be heard on the Paris Bourse during a panic. The kalian was of course in requisition. At it, the more sedate of the Persians and Turks assembled on the balconies whiffed, and looked down unmoved on the excited and shouting throng below. To me also the pipe brought contentment. Stretched on my rug, which I had placed in a corner of the balcony, I gave myself up to the spirit of the scene and enjoyed the luxury of a truly Oriental indolence. In an hour or two I was roused from my dreams by a summons from the palace. It was found, as I had conjectured, that there was ample room there both for Hagee and myself, and for it I abandoned the caravansary reluctantly, but still unwilling to separate myself from the party who were for some days longer to be my fellow-travellers.

Resolved to have a few days' sport on the lagune before leaving Enzelli, I directed Hagee overnight to purchase for me a gun, if such a thing could be had in the town. He succeeded in procuring a double-barrel one, not bad of its kind, but the largest shot which he could get was not equal to what is known to English sportsmen as No. 5. We accordingly started early next morning, and made our way to the wharf, where a boat which Hagee had already chartered was in waiting for us. The boat was large, and seeing some of the muleteers and the Hindoo who had come with the Mission Caravan from Teheran on the wharf, I invited them to join us in our sail, which they were only too happy to do. The sun was very hot, but the after-part of the boat was protected by an awning of mat, and as a further luxury Hagee had brought some ice which he had obtained at the bazaar. The excursion was a very pleasant one. A gentle breeze was blowing, and the barest ripple could be heard at her bows as the boat rose and sank on the swell which was lazily rolling up the lagune. Myriads of birds were to be seen, as on the previous day. With proper ammunition I could in half an hour have made a full bag, but the shot was too small to enable me to do more than flutter them, and enjoy their flight as they winged their way in black masses to other and more secure haunts. Fatigued by the excitement of loading and firing, I stripped and plunged into the water for a swim. Hagee followed, and then with a rush came the Bombay Hindoo and the muleteers, who struck out in a way which much surprised me. I had often occasion to notice, not at Aden alone, but at several other places, the wonderful skill of the natives as swimmers. On the voyage from Bombay to Bushire it was often difficult to land in boats at the stations at which we called, owing to the heavy sea and the surf on the shore, but our deck passengers made light of the matter. Jumping from the ship, they would boldly strike out for the shore, and in no instance did they fail to reach it. I thoroughly admired their pluck and skill, which I attributed to their living close to the sea, and the early age at which they learn to swim. But my wonder was great when I saw the Persian muleteers likewise take to the water and disport themselves in it as if it were their native element. Where could they have learnt the art? I could not explain it. The only water which I saw as I traversed the country, save the rivers which were crossed at long intervals, were the tanks in the compounds; but it was impossible to suppose that they could have been used for the purposes of bathing. Still, there were the muleteers rolling and tumbling, as expert as if they had made the art of swimming their daily practice, and with a fearlessness which could be born only of conscious skill.

A challenge from Hagee to race with me to an island about four hundred yards off roused all my spirit as a Briton, and was at once accepted. One—two—three, and away. We stuck well together until within fifty yards of the island, when I drew away from him and won by about five yards. We were both blown, for the race was a quick one, but would not admit it, and almost immediately started again for the boat. I took the lead, but Hagee soon came up and passed me. A spurt on my part brought us again level. The excitement in the boat was great, for they were all to profit if Hagee won. Hagee himself, knowing that success would bring him a certain quantity of the Russian spirit "vodka," kept straight for the boat, drawing long and steady strokes. It was difficult and laborious work. The wind was in our teeth, and the sea knocked us about most unmercifully. Some forty yards more remained to be covered. Both of us rallied with what little strength remained to us, both strained every nerve to get the lead, but in vain, and both touched the boat together. It was a dead heat. It was with difficulty that I got on board, and when I did succeed in doing so I had to lie down in the stern from exhaustion. I had not been in the water for months, and found that travel, though it had in other respects braced me, was not the best preparation for swimming a match of over eight hundred yards in a rough sea. Though victory lay in the balance between us, I magnanimously gave judgment against myself, and if my opponent had not the glory he and his backers had at least the profit of the race. After we had rested for some time and enjoyed the luxury of the pipe, we landed on an island inhabited by a number of fishermen whom we found mending their nets. Our stay was not long, for at the door of one of the huts a woman who was cleaning fish was uncovered, and the moment our gaze was directed towards her, her husband came forward and remonstrated with such vehemence against our indecent conduct, that I repressed all farther curiosity and beat a hasty retreat. Next morning I strolled along the beach, which is composed of fine sand and shells, and joined a number of Persians, who were bathing in the water. They did not venture any distance out, and I fortunately imitated their example, for I afterwards learned that there is a strong under-current along this shore of the Caspian Sea, and that swimmers perished when caught in it. Enzelli

I found on the whole a very pleasant place. It was sufficiently picturesque to gratify the eye, and its active commerce lent excitement to a visit to the harbour or bazaar. The harbour is a natural one, but is only calculated to afford accommodation to vessels of small tonnage. It was filled during the few days I stayed at the place with fishing boats and a number of Russian schooners, which looked frail craft to contend against the waves of the stormy Caspian. A lighthouse, old and decayed, stands at the entrance, but is only lit up when ships are expected.

The firing of a gun was the signal that our steamer had arrived. My packing was soon done, but I still lingered at the palace, for it had proved an agreeable retreat. The perfume from its garden at night and in the early morning was so delicious that, in the desire to enjoy it, sleep was forgotten; and if repose were the object, the balcony which extended round the building invited to it and the kalian. Here some of our party were always to be found, veritable lotus-eaters, forgetting, in the loveliness of the scene and the enjoyment of the hour, the fatigues which they had so recently undergone. The Persian drum or tom-tom alone disturbed our rest; but against this was to be set the shouts and laughter of children, the only joyous sound which I had heard between the two seas—the Persian Gulf and the Caspian. Enzelli was an agreeable change from Bushire, Shiraz, Ispahan, and Teheran, and though homeward bound, I left it with a feeling akin to regret. I had also to part with Hagee. Like all his class, he had his faults; but he had, nevertheless, been a good and useful servant, though occasionally giving way to his weakness—love for drink. He had, moreover, been the companion of my travels; and the feeling of attachment which grows out of fatigues and dangers shared in common had sprung up between us. I was, therefore, loth to part with him. I readily gave him the "character" which I considered he deserved, and settled the account between us in a way which made him grateful and happy, and compensated him in some measure for his love unrequited by Sarah. She had gone on board early with the Mission Caravan, and when I next saw her she was methodically aiding Mr. A. in ticking off in a small pocketbook the numerous trunks and other articles of baggage which were being lowered into the hold. Hagee accompanied me to the steamer, and insisted upon performing a last act of service by tugging at an oar and leading the boatmen's chorus of " Alli—Alli—All—i." Thus stimulated they bent to their task, and we soon reached the steamer, which lay at anchor off the harbour. Ere long the order was given for all, save the crew and passengers, to leave the decks. But Hagee lingered to the last. He seized my hand and repeatedly kissed it, and tears trickled down his cheeks as he got over the ship's side. I had no idea that there was so much tenderness and affection in his nature, and responded, with an emotion which I could not well conceal, to his cry of " three times three for Mr. Brittlebank," with a " hip, hip, hurrah ! " which caused the Russian officers to think that they had got a lunatic on board with them.

The order was given to steam ahead, and Enzelli quickly receded from our view. But before leaving Persia, a few words as to my disbursements in travelling through it may not be out of place. The hire of horses and mules varied, as may be surmised, according to the character of the district. For three mules hired at Bushire, for the journey to Shiraz, I paid 120 khrans—60 in advance, and 60 on completion of the journey, in addition to the customary present or gratuity to the muleteers; and I paid 157½ khrans for horses from Ispahan to Teheran. I had, in every case, to feed the animals myself; and the charge for provisions and fodder varied from 14 to 20 khrans per day. My daily personal expenses did not, on an average, exceed 12 khrans, the value of the khran being, as I have stated, about 10½*d*, or, say, a franc.

Chapter XV.

ENZELLI TO ASTRAKHAN—NIJNI NOVGOROD.

OUR steamer, a paddle-boat, was about 500 tons burden, and, as far as I could judge, of English build. Her engines were unmistakeably English; she was schooner-rigged, and was in every respect a first-class boat. Her main saloon, in which there were two pianos for the use of the lady passengers, was as beautifully decorated and fitted up as any of the Peninsular and Oriental Company's steamers, and was lighted by swing lamps at night and by large ports in the day. Two tiers of sofas were carried round the saloon, and adjoining it were six state rooms—three on each side —which were reserved for females. So far as completeness of fittings could go there was everything which could conduce to a comfortable passage. Our passengers were a very mixed lot, but Persians and Russians predominated. Happily a member of the Indo-European Telegraph Company's staff who had been for some time stationed at Teheran was also on board. We soon became intimate, and passed the time pleasantly in smoking cigarettes and drinking tea, which the Russians know so well how to make, and in detailing our respective experiences of Persia and Persian travel. The living on board the steamer was after the Russian fashion. With the tea they seldom used milk and only a little sugar, but what I liked most were the delicacies which were taken before the principal meals by way of improving the appetite. Besides caviare, they included diminutive slices of different kinds of strong flavoured sausages and cheese, preserved fish, &c., which are eaten with thin slices of bread and butter about the size of half-a-crown. These condiments were generally laid at the head of the table and were flanked by rows of bottles containing various kinds of "vodka," which I confess I much relished. One old familiar dish never appeared on the table—I mean the

"Irish stew" of all English sea-going ships—and I also missed the curries which had been my chief food in Ceylon, India and Persia.

The Caspian Sea, through which we were now steaming, is about 700 miles in length and from 100 to 270 miles broad. It has no apparent outlet, and its surplus water, which must be very great, inasmuch as it receives the discharge of several large rivers, among them the Volga, is supposed to escape by a subterranean passage into the Persian Gulf. Many arguments are adduced in support of this theory, not the least cogent being the effect of a west wind on the sea itself. With the wind from this quarter—the west—the water perceptibly rises, and it is urged that this result is due to the obstruction which the water then finds to its passage down the hidden channel. But however that may be there is good reason for supposing that at one time the sea extended farther north than it now does. In this direction there is a long belt of sandy and saline plains backed by land covered with vegetation, and their presence is accounted for by the assumption that at some remote period they formed part of the bed of the sea. It has no tide, but its navigation is rendered difficult by sand banks and shallows. In consequence of these, vessels drawing more than twelve feet of water cannot safely sail on it. I tasted the water at several places, and could detect only a very slight saline flavour in it. Many varieties of fish, including the salmon, are found in it, and its shores teem with heron, bitterns, and other kinds of aquatic birds. Like the other seas and rivers of Russia, it is blocked up during the winter months, but the ice disappears about the end of March, and navigation and fishing are then resumed.

On the day following our departure we arrived at Astara, a frontier station between Persia and Russia. We came to about a mile from the shore, and took in some passengers, most of whom were Persians. A few hours' more steaming brought us abreast of Lankeran, which seemed to be embowered in trees, and looked pretty from the sea. Sunday, the 20th of May, found us at Baku. It looked a thriving place. It has extensive quays, and among the number of sailing vessels which were ranged along them were two Russian war steamers, looking far more trim than one would suppose a Russian man-of-war would be in this lonely sea. The town lies on the west coast of the Caspian. The population includes, besides Russians, Armenians, and Persians, a few Germans; and naphtha and rock-salt are largely exported from it. My friend and myself went ashore with the intention of breakfasting at a café, where we had to intimate our wants by signs; but the food offered us was so bad—a perfect mess, in fact—that we returned to the steamer for our morning meal. After breakfast we again went on shore, and strolled about the town. The shops were poor for a place of so much trade; but the dress of the better class of people indicated comfort and affluence. A public garden, to which we were attracted by the musical strains of a brass band, was crowded with them, sauntering up and down like the visitors at a German watering-place. Very few women were present, and these were dressed with a taste and elegance which it would be difficult to surpass. The military element abounded; and its organization as a Russian town could not, of course, be complete without its detectives and spies. One of these gentlemen paid us special attention, following us wherever we went, and accompanying us even to the ship's side when we returned on board. Our stroll had also other drawbacks. The heat of the sun was overpowering, the streets were dusty, and the "droshkies" dashed furiously along them, the drivers having apparently as little regard for their cattle as for foot-passengers. It was late when we returned to the steamer, but the visits to the officers by their citizen friends, which had commenced shortly after we had come alongside the quay, were not yet over. Scarcely had one party of them left than another came on board; and so the day passed in greeting and merry-making. How the officers managed to bear the expense of such oppressive acquaintanceship I know not, unless, as in the case of Government ships, an allowance is made to them for entertaining. Having shipped a good many passengers, we resumed our voyage on the 27th. The wind had risen over night, and we had a lively time of it at sea; but having now got my "sea-legs," my sufferings were confined to want of sleep, owing to the difficulty of holding on to my sofa during the pitching and rolling of the ship. It was otherwise with my fellow passengers. The sounds familiar to the voyager on a bad passage between Calais and Dover were unceasing during the night, and at breakfast and dinner there were many vacant places at the table.

The last night we were to be on board, my friend and myself dined, by invitation, with the engineers. The bill-of-fare was excellent, so was the "vodka," so were the cigarettes; and our sitting was prolonged into the small hours, when one of those sudden and terrible squalls, which are common to the Caspian as to the Black Sea, struck the ship. It was happily as brief as it was sudden; but the uproar which it occasioned in the saloon was something to be remembered. Several of the passengers were pitched right on to the floor from the sofas, and an old Russian officer, who with difficulty clung to his berth, was the Job's comforter of the occasion, consoling the sufferers by the assurance that the worst was yet to come. Like other prophets of evil, however, his predictions happily were not fulfilled. Our ship rode gallantly through the storm, and about 3 P.M. on the 29th we ranged alongside the barge which was waiting our arrival to take us up to Astrakhan, the steamer's draught being too great to allow her to cross the bar which obstructs the entrance to the port. The barge was of large size—capable, indeed, of carrying quite as many passengers as the steamer herself—and was provided with a saloon and cabins, clean but hot. A good table was also kept on board, the caviare, which forms an article of trade on the lower Volga, and especially at Astrakhan, being particularly good and fresh. It is made principally from the roe of the sturgeon; but other fish are also used for the purpose. The roe of these is small as compared with that of the sturgeon, from which as much as twenty-five pounds can be obtained, and is used in the preparation of the common pressed caviare. In making it, the coarse strings and fibres are first removed from the roe; it is then salted and spread out on mats to dry, which, in fine weather, takes about six hours. After this it is trodden with the feet, which are covered with leather stockings, and is then placed in butts. The best caviare is known as "sack caviare," which, to the eye, appears to consist solely of the eggs of the roe. After undergoing the cleansing process already mentioned, it is steeped in brine until the grains become quite soft; it is then hung up in long, narrow, pointed bags, on the top of which brine is poured, and is so kept until the water has all oozed out. When dry it is trodden into and stored away in casks. Our passengers now included several Tartars, and we had also on board a number of Russian prisoners on their way to the penal settlements of Siberia. Their hands were tied behind their backs, and they seemed very sad and depressed, as if foreseeing their doom. They were watched day and night, but I did not observe that their guards acted in any cruel spirit towards them. Nothing of any interest occurred during this part of our sail up the Volga. The scenery was tame, almost flat, and the appearance of the villages, which were rather numerous, led me to suppose that the river occasionally overflowed its banks. Our progress was slow, the tug which towed the barge being of small power, so that we did not reach Astrakhan until the 31st. The town was formerly the capital of the province whose name it bears. Its wharves and quays, of which there are many, and all good, were crowded with shipping of small tonnage, and the place had a bustling and thriving look. It contains several churches, monasteries, and schools; and the houses, which are built of wood, bear some resemblance to the log-houses which are to be seen in Canada and America. Its population is considerable. It has a strong Tartar element; but representatives of almost every European nation are to be found amongst its merchants and traders. Its streets are broad, but its shops are not attractive, very few articles of merchandise, and those of poor quality, being displayed in them. Its public garden was, however, well laid out, and seemed the favourite resort of the better class of the inhabitants, who appeared prosperous and were well dressed.

We left Astrakhan on the 1st of June. At this point the sail up the Volga may be said to commence. The steamer which was to take us up stream was an excellent one of her kind, and bore a family resemblance to those which run on the Hudson and the new class of Rhine boats—smaller than the one, larger than the other. Her engines were magnificent specimens of English workmanship, and drove her up against the current at the rate of eleven knots an hour. Her fittings were superb. The first-class saloon was like a drawing-room, the berths were commodious, and all the arrangements were of the luxurious character which distinguishes boat and railway travelling in Russia. My deficiency in the Russian tongue was, however, a sad drawback to my comfort. The stewards could speak neither French nor German, nothing, in fact, but Russian—a very unusual circumstance—and I had to make my wants known by signs and gestures, which were not always as successful as I could wish. My first difficulty arose on getting on board after a walk through Astrakhan, in which I lost my way. I only reached the quay as the steamer was on the point of starting, and was famished from exertion and long fasting. I strove to make the steward understand my condition, but in vain. At last, observing a Russian eating beefsteak, I pointed to his plate and then to my mouth. I was promptly served. So far so good. But now sprang up another torment, for whenever I again signified a desire for food or looked hungry, lo! there was the steward with the typical dish of my country. Beefsteak, beefsteak, and nothing but beefsteak until the end of the voyage! He had probably learned that it was the dish prized above all by Englishmen, and he smiled approval whenever he laid it before me. I cannot say that I quite appreciated the compliment, and was unpatriotic enough to desire a change.

My friends and fellow-travellers in Persia disembarked at Tzaritzin, where the steamer stopped to take in wood. Vienna was the route by which they intended to return to England, and this was the point at which they were to branch off for the most enjoyable capital in Europe. After I had assisted them to get their luggage ashore—no easy matter—and taken leave of them, I watched the men and women as they brought on board the wood which is used for fuel, and which is stored ready cut in large piles at the different stations, and then went into the town, which, like the other Russian towns I had seen on the river, possessed a public garden. It was as usual full of citizens listening to the music of an excellent band, which appeared to be as much an institution in the towns on the Volga as on the Rhine. It was late when we resumed our voyage. It was blowing fresh against the stream, and what might be termed a heavy sea was running, deluging the deck with spray, and causing the boat to heave and toss as she would under like circumstances in the English Channel. I stood in the bow for some time noting the height of the waves, but I found the situation too exposed, and removed to the deck-house. As the night advanced the wind increased to a full gale. It also became very dark, and, ere long, we were unpleasantly made aware of the dangers attending the navigation of the river. On looking ahead after I had been for an hour or two on the deck-house, and straining my eyes to pierce the darkness, I thought I could descry an object some distance off on the port bow. I supposed it at first to be a rock, and that its position was well known to those on board, but as we drew nearer I could see that it was a large sailing barge close hauled, and that she was crossing our bows. There was yet time to clear her if the helm were at once ported. But the men at the wheel, who were out of hearing, even if it were possible for me to make them understand, did not yet observe her. When they did, the steam whistle sent forth its shrill cry, the engines were reversed and the helm put hard aport, but too late. A moment more, and the steamer struck the barge with great force, knocking a man, who appeared on her deck just before the collision, and who was frantically gesticulating, off his feet, and, as it was feared at the time, into the river. The barge passed rapidly astern and was lost in the darkness. The commotion on board the steamer was terrible. The force of the collision was so great that all feared she had suffered serious damage, and the passengers came rushing on deck in the wildest confusion and alarm. The engines, which were going full speed astern were soon stopped, and the steamer having lost way rolled about in a manner which added much to the terrors of the women and those unaccustomed to the sea. Like the Rhine steamers, she carried only one small boat, the knowledge of which fact was not calculated to allay the confusion or excite confidence. The boat was lowered, and was manned by some of the crew, who pulled away after the barge. Their task was both a difficult and a dangerous one. The wind was dead ahead, the waves were high, and I expected every moment to see her swamped. She too passed out of sight, and our suspense became painful. The terror of the women was almost infectious. With others of the male passengers, I sought to allay it as we best could. One device had a good effect. Calling to mind the story of the officer in battle, who seeing his men on the point of becoming panic-stricken, coolly took a cigar from his case and proceeded to light and smoke it, and so restored their courage, I went into the saloon, and affecting a confidence which I did not feel, lighted a cigarette and smoked with a seeming relish of its fragrance. My apparent coolness—I may now confess that it was more apparent than real, and that I was seriously alarmed for our situation— was accepted as an assurance of safety, and there was some cessation in the cries and lamentations which had previously filled the saloon. The circumstance which alarmed me the most, and also astonished me, was the neglect of our own crew to ascertain the extent of the damage done to the steamer. They did not seem to give it a thought, but I could not make out whether the neglect of their first and most ordinary duty under the circumstances was due to faith in the strength of the vessel, indifference, or the loss of the power of reflection in the general commotion.

Our damage, as it fortunately turned out, was not serious, but the incident made such an impression on me, that whenever during the remainder of the trip I heard the engines stop or the whistle blow at night, I took the precaution to come on deck and see for myself how matters stood. The boat returned in about an hour, and reported that the barge had been seriously damaged, but that those on board hoped to reach their port of destination, which was two miles farther down the river, before she sank, and that no life had been lost. It further appeared that at the time of the collision her crew were all asleep.

Things assumed their wonted appearance on board the steamer, and we again proceeded to steam rapidly up stream. The down boat could always be tracked at night by the showers of fiery sparks discharged from her funnel. Running with the current her speed was always great, and scarcely would she be sighted than she would rush past us, her saloon and cabins all ablaze with light. These were the nightly incidents, but though exciting for the moment, they lessened only in a slight degree the monotony of the voyage. Kazan, which in most respects resembled

Astrakhan, was also called at, and on the 7th June we reached Nijni Novgorod, beyond which the steamer does not ascend. The Volga is not without its beauty in respect of natural scenery. Towards its mouth its banks are flat, and its waters spread over the country, forming pools and marshes; but it narrows as you ascend, its banks grow steep, and dense woods which come down to the water's edge give it a picturesque effect, especially at night, when their shadows are relieved by the lights of the passing steamer. It can, however, in no way compare with the Rhine or the Hudson. It has not the variety of the one, or the bluffs and headlands, the swift current and mighty volume, of the other.

Chapter XVI.

HOME.

MY stay at Nijni Novgorod extended only to a few hours. The scene of its great fair, which is held in July every year, was quite deserted, and I could see no indication of the bustle and excitement with which in a few weeks the town would be filled. At the railway station I by good fortune fell in with a gentleman who understood French. With his assistance I was able to obtain all that I required both in the town and on the journey to Moscow, and should these lines ever meet his eye I beg to assure him that his kindness and attention have not been forgotten. The train left the station at 4 P.M. and arrived at Moscow next morning, the 8th, at 7 A.M., the journey occupying fifteen hours. The carriages resembled those on the Swiss lines, but were much more comfortable, every first-class passenger having an arm-chair, which he could lengthen by three feet or so by means of a leg-rest whenever he wished to recline or slumber. I had heard that the train was also provided with sleeping carriages, but was unable to secure a berth. On reaching Moscow I jumped into a vehicle, and drove to Dusseaux's Hotel. My request for a room was met with some hesitation. I felt somewhat indignant at it, but a moment's reflection showed me that it was not unreasonable. Neither my appearance nor my luggage vouched for my respectability. Sunburnt and travel-stained, a broad-brimmed felt hat, covered by a "puggary" to conceal its shabbiness, ornamenting my head, a costume on the whole rather scanty, and my tangled hair, which had grown to a preposterous length, hanging down to my shoulders, I might have presented myself on any stage and passed for an Italian brigand or Mexican robber.

This reading of my character was borne out by my kit, which was all rolled up in a water-proof sheet, and looked a poor guarantee for a long bill. Realizing the situation, I looked as important as I possibly could, and

repeating my demand for a room, added—
"By the way, has General So-and-So yet arrived?" The effect was wonderful. A *militaire* my friend, and he a general! No doubt an Anglais *milord* in disguise. My pedlar's pack swelled to the proportion of a field marshal's baggage, and I no longer appeared the kind of guest who would be likely to appropriate the silver spoons. The waiters ceased to grin; their chief stepped forward and bowed me to my room, and then retired to see if the name of my distinguished friend the general was on their list. I was much concerned to hear that he had not arrived after his solemn promise, given at Ceylon and renewed in India, to meet me in Moscow on this very day, but still bore up against the disappointment. A wash and a bath, to which I had for some time been a stranger, followed by a good dinner, revived my drooping spirits and prepared me for a visit to the shops of the town in search of clothes and other articles which I required, but which I found great difficulty in obtaining. My impression on returning to the hotel was that Moscow must be the paradise of bill-posters. Every shop was covered with

an illustrated advertisement indicating the things which might be purchased within. The streets were lined with these mural decorations, but the effect was not of a kind which would please a severe art critic. The famous Kremlin fortress stands in a central part of the town, which, though quaint, does not impress the visitor. Some of its suburbs, however, are very beautiful, and the villas, which are all magnificent, assume in some instances the dimensions of small palaces. The great feature of the town is its churches, with their lofty domes and large gilt crosses. It can boast, I think, of a larger number of such edifices than any Italian city with which I am acquainted ; and if its population be not holy, it certainly is not from want of opportunity to practise their devotions. The " big bell of Moscow" is of course also one of its sights, and I might add the object likewise of its reverence. The weight of the metal monster exceeds 198 tons. Its height is 19 ft., its circumference at the bottom 63 ft. 11 in., and its greatest thickness 23 in. It narrowly escaped destruction in 1737, when it fell to the ground, carrying everything before it, owing to the burning of the beams from which it was suspended. It was again hoisted with infinite labour by means of powerful tackle to its original position, where it now hangs, but no longer sends forth its thunder-peal far and wide over the city. Both here and at St. Petersburg, as well as at all the towns at which we stopped on the Volga, I was struck by the courtesy which the people showed one to another. No matter how humble, politeness marked their intercourse. Even the beggars saluted each other by taking off the hat, and parted with profound bows. It may only be a thin veneering of French polish, but the habit is not without its advantages, and is certainly pleasant to behold.

Leaving Moscow at 8 p.m. on the 9th, I arrived at St. Petersburg at 11 a.m. on the 10th of June. The country through which the railway passed reminded me very much of some of the Western States of America; and so close was the resemblance sometimes, that had I been suddenly dropped down in the place, I could not have said in which of the two continents I was. A tedious journey brought me to Berlin, and thence to Calais, and on the 14th of June, at 6 p.m., I reached London. My tour had been on the whole an enjoyable one. Its dangers and fatigues were soon forgotten. The recollection of its pleasures has been revived by the preparation of my narrative, and excites anew the love for wandering. My pack is ready. I intend soon to shoulder it again, and hope to hear from the reader a kind " Bon voyage!"

THE END.

www.ingramcontent.com/pod-product-compliance
Lightning Source LLC
Chambersburg PA
CBHW031933230426
43672CB00010B/1912